INCREDIBLE
EDIBLE
SCIENCE

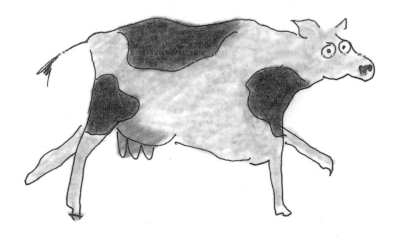

For my son, Josh,
whom I love more than chocolate

—T. L. S.

Text copyright © 1994 Tina L. Seelig.
Illustrations copyright © 1994 W. H. Freeman and Company.
All rights reserved.

Scientific American Books for Young Readers is an imprint of
W. H. Freeman and Company,
41 Madison Avenue, New York, New York 10010.

Book design by Debora Smith

Library of Congress Cataloging–in–Publication Data

Seelig, Tina Lynn.
Incredible edible science/ Tina L. Seelig; illustrations by Lynn Brunelle. Includes index.
ISBN 0–7167–6501–2 (hard). — ISBN 0–7167–6507–1 (soft)
1. Cookery—Juvenile literature. 2. Food—Juvenile literature.
[1. Cookery. 2. Food.] I. Brunelle, Lynn, ill. II. Title.
TX652.5.S42 1994
641.5—dc20

93–33480
CIP
AC

Printed in the United States of America
10 9 8 7 6 5 4 3 2 1

Note: Neither the publisher nor the author shall be liable for any damage that may be caused or any injury sustained as a result of doing any of the recipes or other activities in this book.

"INCREDIBLE EDIBLE SCIENCE"

Tina L. Seelig

illustrations by Lynn Brunelle

Scientific American
BOOKS FOR YOUNG READERS

W. H. FREEMAN   NEW YORK

CONTENTS

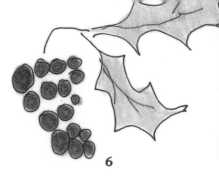

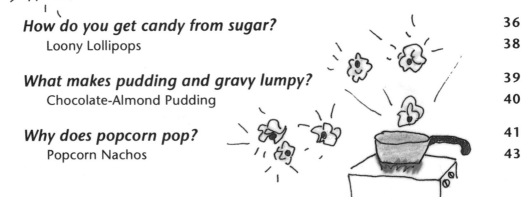

CONTENTS

INTRODUCTION

Have you ever thought of your kitchen as a chemistry laboratory? They may look very different but when you cook, you use many of the same methods that chemists use in a laboratory.

Both cooks and lab scientists measure and combine ingredients. They both heat, cool, shake, and stir their mixtures. They both keep careful track of all the steps they take—the recipe—so that they can repeat the steps later. And when they see changes that have occurred in their ingredients, they both ask, "How did that happen?"

Have you ever wondered why onions make you cry when you cut them? Why oil and water don't mix? Why popcorn pops? These cooking mysteries and many others have puzzled people for years. But science can answer these questions—and so can you!

Each section of this book asks a question about cooking that you may have wondered. It leads you through a scientific investigation to find the answer. And it finishes with a delicious recipe that demonstrates some of the scientific principles at work. Take the time to think about the scientific principles. Try the recipes. Then experiment with recipes of your own, based on your new understanding.

Remember:

- *Like a chemistry laboratory, a kitchen can be a dangerous place. Obey all safety rules.*

- *Unless you are an experienced cook and have permission to use the kitchen, get an adult to help you use the stove, the oven, or any dangerous cooking utensil. Use ovenproof mitts or pot holders whenever you handle hot objects.*

- *If you don't understand a term, look it up in the glossary at the back of the book.*

- *And, finally, don't forget to clean up!*

COOKING UTENSILS

At the top of each recipe you'll find little drawings like these that show you what cooking utensils you need.

Frying pan (skillet)

Cutting board

Jar with lid

Measuring cups

Saucepan (pot)

Sieve

Electric mixer or hand beater

Knife

Fork

Slotted spoon

Bowl

Pastry brush

Stirring spoon

Measuring spoons

Skewers

Wire rack

Rolling pin

Deep fat/candy thermometer

Container with lid

Square pan (8- or 9-inch)

Oven thermometer

Muffin tin

Pizza pan

Thermos

Baking sheet

Cheesecloth

SOLUTIONS

When you cook, chemical reactions take place. Most of these chemical reactions occur in solutions. What is a solution? It is a mixture of ingredients in which one or more ingredients dissolves—breaks up—in a liquid.

Try adding a teaspoon of table salt to a cup of water. If you stir the water, the salt disappears. Where does it go? The salt has dissolved. It has formed a chemical relationship with the water. This means they won't separate on their own. The easiest way to separate them is to boil away the water, changing it into a gas and leaving the salt behind.

But not all ingredients dissolve in all liquids. Try adding a teaspoon of flour to a cup of water. Does the flour dissolve? No. This is because flour particles do not form a chemical relationship with the water. However, they are suspended—held up—by the water molecules for a short time. This kind of mixture is called a suspension. Eventually, the flour will fall down to the bottom of the cup.

Finally, try adding a teaspoon of oil to a cup of water. What happens? They quickly separate because oil and water are so different that they cannot be mixed. The oil rises to the top of the cup.

In this section you will discover some useful things about solutions:

- *Why a liquid boils.*

- *How its boiling point can be changed.*

- *How you can change the freezing point of a solution.*

- *What the difference is between fat and oil.*

- *How you can trick oil and water into mixing.*

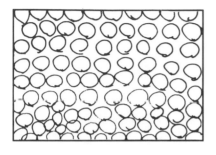

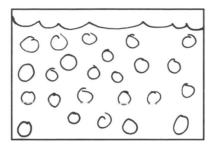

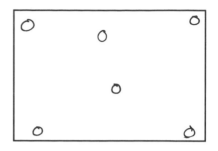

| Solid | Liquid | Gas |

Quick Chemistry

All matter (everything that has weight and takes up space) is made up of about 100 substances called elements. All elements are made up of tiny atoms, which are far too small to be seen even under a microscope. The atoms in an element join together to form longer units called molecules.

Sometimes atoms join together with atoms of another element and form a kind of molecule called a compound. This is an entirely new substance. For example, two atoms of the element hydrogen and one atom of the element oxygen make up a molecule of water. Sugar is made up of several carbon, hydrogen, and oxygen atoms. Some molecules are made up of hundreds of atoms.

Matter can be found in three different states: solid, liquid, and gas. Particles in a solid are strongly attracted to one another, so they don't move around much. A solid has a definite shape and volume (amount of space it takes up). Particles in a liquid are less strongly attracted, so they move and slide over one another. A liquid has no definite shape, but its volumes stays the same. Gas particles are only weakly attracted to one another, so they spread out to fill any size container they're in.

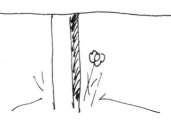

Why does water boil?

Have you ever heard the saying "A watched pot never boils"? Well, a watched pot *always* boils—if it reaches a high enough temperature. But what is boiling and why does it happen?

A single teaspoon of water is made up of billions of water molecules that are constantly moving. Some move so fast that they evaporate—bounce out of the liquid and enter the air as water vapor, a gas. This goes on all the time, but you can't see it. If left long enough, all the water in the teaspoon will evaporate.

The water molecules that evaporate push upward on the air above the teaspoon. This is called the vapor pressure. The air above the teaspoon pushes down on the water. This is called the atmospheric pressure because it is the weight of all the air directly above the teaspoon.

When you heat a pot of water on the stove, the water molecules move faster and faster. The hotter the water, the faster they escape into the air. When the water is pushing upward as hard as the air is pushing back, the water boils. The water bubbles and swirls and even makes noise.

The boiling temperature of water at sea level is 212°F (100°C). No matter how much you heat the water, it can't get hotter than its boiling point. Cooking food in rapidly boiling water does not cook food any faster than cooking it at a low boil. It just causes the water to boil away more quickly. That's why many recipes tell you to turn the heat down to a simmer after the liquid boils—to keep it at the boiling point without boiling away all the liquid.

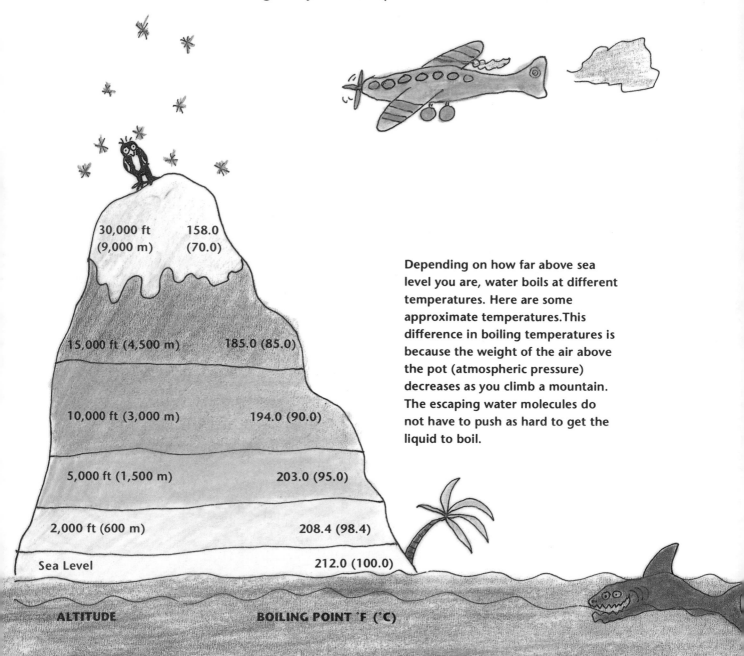

Depending on how far above sea level you are, water boils at different temperatures. Here are some approximate temperatures. This difference in boiling temperatures is because the weight of the air above the pot (atmospheric pressure) decreases as you climb a mountain. The escaping water molecules do not have to push as hard to get the liquid to boil.

30,000 ft (9,000 m)	158.0 (70.0)
15,000 ft (4,500 m)	185.0 (85.0)
10,000 ft (3,000 m)	194.0 (90.0)
5,000 ft (1,500 m)	203.0 (95.0)
2,000 ft (600 m)	208.4 (98.4)
Sea Level	212.0 (100.0)
ALTITUDE	**BOILING POINT °F (°C)**

Different liquids boil at different temperatures. The temperature at which a liquid boils depends on how strong the bonds (links) are between the atoms and between the molecules in the liquid.

SUBSTANCE	BOILING POINT °F (°C) at sea level	
Iodine (antiseptic for cuts)	363.8	(184.4)
Water	212.0	(100.0)
Rubbing Alcohol	180.3	(82.4)
Propane (fuel for grills)	−43.8	(−42.1)

WARNING: Do not try to boil any of these liquids except water!

You can cook many different kinds of foods, such as eggs, vegetables, and grains, in boiling liquid. People all over the world cook grains to eat as hot cereal, a side dish, a main course, or even dessert. In all of these dishes, the grain absorbs the boiling liquid. Here are some delicious recipes.

2 cups water

2 tablespoons butter or margarine

1/2 teaspoon salt

1 cup couscous

3/4 cup raisins

1 teaspoon cinnamon

Surprising Cereal—Couscous

This delicious grain (pronounced KOOSS-kooss), a specialty of North Africa, is made from semolina, a kind of wheat. This recipe is for hot breakfast cereal, something like Cream of Wheat. With a few changes it can become a side dish at dinner or a dessert. Many supermarkets carry couscous. If you don't find it at yours, try a health food store.

1. In a heavy saucepan, bring the water, the butter, and the salt to a boil.

2. Gradually add the couscous, stirring with a wooden spoon.

3. Continue to boil and stir for about 2 minutes, until the water is almost absorbed.

4. Stir in the raisins and the cinnamon, remove from heat, cover tightly, and let stand for 10 minutes.

5. Fluff with the wooden spoon and dish the couscous into cereal bowls.

6. Serve with milk. Add a little extra salt and some sugar if you want.

Makes 4 servings.

For side dish: If you think the sweet taste will not go with your main course, prepare the couscous as above but don't add the milk, sugar, raisins, and cinnamon. Increase salt to 1 teaspoon. Makes 4 to 6 servings.

For dessert: Prepare as in original recipe. Spoon into 6 dessert dishes. Don't add milk, but sprinkle with cinnamon and more sugar, if you like. Top with whipped cream. Makes 6 servings.

If you'd rather go with the tried and true, here are other suggestions for cooking grains in boiling water.

Oatmeal: Not the so-called instant kind that comes in packets, but the kind you measure out yourself. Follow manufacturer's directions. Then dress it up with your favorite extras—fresh fruit, raisins, brown sugar and cinnamon, honey and almonds, or maple syrup.

Rice: Prepare according to package directions. Store 3 cups cooked rice in the refrigerator until the next day, for the Fancy Fried Rice recipe in this book. Or for a different breakfast treat, spoon into cereal bowls and add raisins, sprinkle with 1/4 teaspoon cinnamon, pour in milk, and add sugar to taste.

How do you make ice cream?

"I scream, you scream, we all scream for ice cream!" Almost everyone loves ice cream. It is a mixture of a few simple ingredients: cream, sugar, and flavoring. But if you just toss them together and put them in the freezer, you don't get the rich taste and firm but light texture. What's the secret?

Three things have to happen when you make ice cream:

- *The water in the cream must freeze solid into tiny ice crystals. The crystals make the ice cream firm.*

- *The mixture must be whipped in order to mix in tiny air bubbles. The bubbles make the ice cream light.*

- *The fat in the cream must coat the ice crystals and the air bubbles. The fat makes the ice cream rich and creamy.*

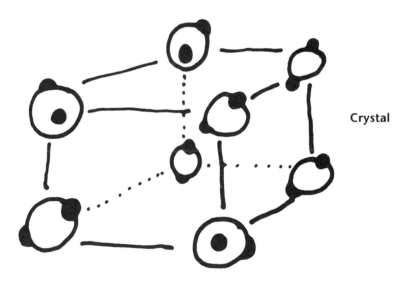

Crystal

When water freezes, it forms regular patterns called ice crystals.

The most important thing to know about making ice cream is that when you dissolve the sugar in the cream, it lowers the temperature at which the water in the cream freezes—forms ice crystals—below its usual freezing temperature of 32°F (0°C). The more sugar in the mixture, the lower the freezing point. In order to make the ice cream freeze, you have to lower the temperature of the mixture. How do you do that?

For years, home ice-cream makers have been available. The oldest kind has three main parts:

- *An inner canister into which the mixture of cream and sugar is placed.*

- *A paddle (or dasher) inside the canister that turns, in order to whip air into the ice cream and to break the forming ice into tiny crystals. The paddles always used to be turned by hand, but now most are turned electrically.*

- *An outer canister that holds the ice and rock salt, which chill the inner canister.*

Why is salt added to the ice? Because the salt lowers the freezing point of water. The ice melts and the cold water mixes with the salt, forming brine—salty water—that can get much colder than plain water before it freezes. It makes the ice-cream mixture in the canister get colder and colder—until the ice cream freezes.

In recent years, another kind of ice-cream maker has been used too. The freezer contains an alcohol solution instead of salt and ice in its outer canister. The ice-cream maker is placed in the freezer in order to freeze the alcohol solution. Since alcohol freezes at a lower temperature than water, the outer canister is cold enough to freeze the ice cream. Then the paddle method is used to whip the ice cream

Even if you don't have an ice-cream maker, you can still make ice cream—as long as you have a freezer and set it at its coldest setting. By beating some of the ingredients together until they get very fluffy, more air gets into the mixture. You don't use a paddle to mix in air. Although the results may not be quite as good, you will still have a delicious treat. This is called still-frozen ice cream. So if you don't have an ice-cream maker, follow the special directions for still-frozen ice cream at the end of the recipe.

People have been enjoying ice-cream–like desserts for 4,000 years. In China, a favorite food of the rich was milk ice. It was made from a soft paste of rice, spices, and milk, which was then packed in snow. Ice cream traveled to Europe in the 1300s and to the United States with Thomas Jefferson around 1800.

Chocolate-Chip Ice Cream

Ice-cream-maker version

1. In a small saucepan, beat together the eggs, milk, sugar, and salt until well blended.

2. Cook, stirring constantly, over very low heat, until the mixture thickens enough to coat a metal spoon.

3. Cool completely in the refrigerator.

4. Stir in the heavy cream, vanilla, and chocolate chips.

5. Chill in the refrigerator for at least 2 hours.

6. Turn the mixture into the metal canister of an ice-cream maker and freeze according to the manufacturer's directions.

7. Remove the dasher and scoop the ice cream into a 1-quart container. Cover and place in the freezer for 2 to 5 hours. This will make the ice cream harder and allow the flavors to blend.

Makes about 1 quart.

2 eggs

1 cup milk

1/2 cup sugar

1/8 teaspoon salt

1 1/2 cups heavy cream

2 teaspoons vanilla

1/2 cup semi-sweet mini chocolate chips

Still-frozen method

Cook and cool the mixture as in steps 1 to 3 on page 19. In a large bowl, use a mixer to beat the heavy cream and vanilla until stiff peaks form. (To test, turn off the mixer. The cream should hold its shape when the beaters are lifted out of the bowl.) Do not overbeat the cream, or you will make butter. Gently fold the egg mixture into the whipped cream until it is well blended. Gently fold in the chocolate chips. Turn into a 1-quart container. Cover and place in the freezer until the ice cream is firm, about 4 hours. This ice cream will not be as smooth as the ice-cream-maker version.

Mint Chocolate-Chip Ice Cream

Prepare the ice cream as above, substituting 1 teaspoon mint extract for the vanilla. Add 4 drops of green food coloring, if desired, with the extract.

20

What is the difference between fat and oil?

Fat, such as that found on meat, and oil, such as corn or olive oil, are very similar. They are made of the same kind of molecules — but fats are solid at room temperature and oils are liquid. The size and shape of the molecules determines if they are solid or liquid.

Some fat molecules are long and straight, and others are short and bent. The long, straight molecules (saturated fats) stack together easily and form a solid fat. The short, bent fat molecules (unsaturated fats) don't stack easily and are usually liquid at room temperature.

Saturated fat

Saturated Fats The carbon atoms in these fat molecules are "saturated" with hydrogen atoms. This means they have as much hydrogen bound to them as possible. The resulting molecule is straight.

Unsaturated fat

Unsaturated Fats The carbon atoms in these fat molecules are "not saturated" with hydrogen. This means there is less hydrogen than possible. The resulting molecule is bent wherever it is missing hydrogen atoms.

HEY, FATTY!

Animals and plants store fat as an energy supply. Animals store fat throughout their bodies to use when food is scarce. Plants store fat in their seeds to provide fuel for sprouting.

Fancy Fried Rice

2 strips of bacon

1/4 cup peanut or other vegetable oil

1/2 cup chopped onion

2 cloves garlic, chopped or crushed

1 teaspoon freshly grated ginger or 1/4 to 1/2 teaspoon ground ginger

1/2 cup thin-sliced carrots

1 cup quartered and sliced zucchini

1/2 cup fresh or thawed frozen peas

2 eggs, lightly beaten

3 cups cooked rice, preferably one day old

1/4 cup soy sauce

1. In a large frying pan or wok, fry the bacon until the heat changes the fat to liquid and the meat is brown and crisp. Remove the bacon and drain it on paper towels, leaving the bacon drippings in the pan. When the bacon cools, crumble it into small pieces and set aside.

2. Add the peanut oil, onions, garlic, and ginger to the hot bacon drippings. Cook and stir over medium heat until the onions are soft and slightly browned.

3. Add the sliced carrots. Cook and stir until the carrots soften. Add the zucchini and cook and stir until it softens. Add the peas and cook only until they are heated through. Turn off burner. Remove the vegetables from the pan with a slotted spoon and place them in a large bowl.

4. Over medium heat, add the beaten eggs to the hot drippings. Scramble the eggs until they are well cooked. Break them up with the slotted spoon and add them to the bowl with the vegetables.

5. Add the rice to the pan with the hot drippings. Cook and stir until hot. Add the soy sauce and mix well.

6. Add the crumbled bacon and the vegetable-egg mixture to the hot rice. Cook and stir until heated through. Serve immediately.

Makes 4 to 6 servings.

Why don't oil and water mix?

Both oil and water are used in many sauces and salad dressings. You can shake a jar of oil and water from today to tomorrow, but when you stop, they will separate. Why?

It's all in the molecules. Water is made up of polar molecules, which are like magnets. Just as the negative end (pole) of one magnet is attracted to the positive end (pole) of another magnet, the negative side of a polar molecule is attracted to the positive side of another polar molecule.

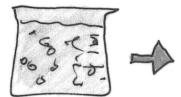

But oil is not made of polar molecules. So instead of attracting the polar water, it is pushed away. But in which direction? Since oil is lighter than water, it naturally rises to the surface.

It is possible to get oil and water to mix by using a third substance that acts as a "peacemaker." The molecules in the peacemaker, called emulsifiers, have two ends, or "hands." One "hand" is water-loving and grabs hold of a water molecule. The other "hand" is water-fearing and grabs hold of an oil molecule. In this way the emulsifier becomes a bridge between the water and the oil.

Common cooking emulsifiers include egg yolk, mustard, yogurt, honey, and dried herbs. Egg yolks are used in making mayonnaise. Mustard is used in making vinaigrette salad dressing.

Oil

Emulsifiers

Water

Here is a delicious recipe for salad dressing. See what happens when you combine the vinegar and the oil. Then add the mustard and watch it all come together.

Honey-Mustard Salad Dressing

2 tablespoons cider vinegar

2 tablespoons vegetable oil

1 tablespoon honey

1 tablespoon Dijon-style mustard

Salt and pepper to taste

1. Place vinegar and oil in a small jar with a tight lid.
2. Shake well and see what happens.
3. Add honey and mustard and shake. See the difference?
4. Add salt and pepper to taste. Shake before pouring over your favorite salad vegetables.

Makes about 1/3 cup.

24

ACIDS AND BASES

Did you know that you eat acids and bases all the time? You eat an acid whenever you chomp on a pickle or sip hot chocolate. You eat a base whenever you bite into the white part of an egg. In fact, all foods can be described as acidic, basic, or neutral. Knowing the differences can tell you a lot about how ingredients will react with each other.

You can tell how acidic or basic some foods are by tasting them. For example, vinegar and lemon juice, which are both quite acidic, are sour. Water is neutral and has no strong taste unless strong-tasting chemicals, used to keep germs out, are added. Baking soda, which is basic, tastes bitter.

The amount of acid or base in a substance can be measured on a special scale called pH. The scale goes from 1 to 14, with 7 as neutral. The more acidic the substance, the lower the number on the pH scale. The more basic the substance, the higher the number on the pH scale. (Another word often used for *basic* is *alkaline*.) When acids and bases are mixed together in the right amounts, they can neutralize each other.

In highly acidic solutions proteins change shape, and long sugars such as starch break apart into small pieces.

In the following sections you will see how acids or bases:

- *Help batter rise.*

- *Prevent cut fruits from browning.*

- *Turn cucumbers into pickles.*

What is the difference between baking soda and powder?

When you make cakes, muffins, or biscuits, the recipes always call for baking soda or baking powder. If you try to make these recipes without baking soda or baking powder, you will probably end up with an inedible mess. Why? Because they make your batter rise. But they are used under different conditions. What are those conditions?

Baking soda is a base. It is used in batters containing acidic liquid ingredients such as lemon juice, buttermilk, yogurt, sour cream, pineapple juice, molasses, melted chocolate, and vinegar. The baking soda and the acid react chemically, neutralizing each other and releasing carbon dioxide gas. The gas is trapped as bubbles in the batter.

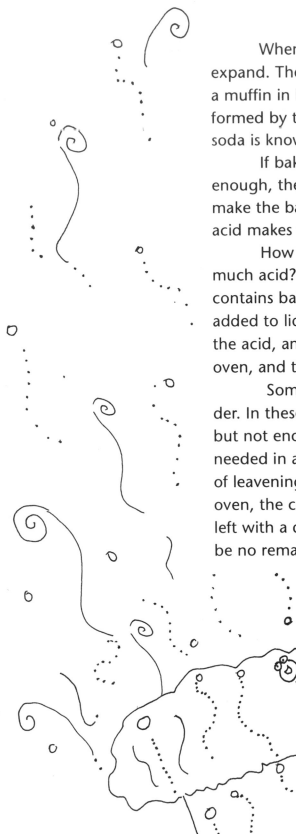

When the batter is placed in a hot oven, the bubbles expand. The batter expands around them, making it rise. Cut a muffin in half and look at all the little holes. They were formed by this process, which is called leavening. The baking soda is known as the leavening agent.

If baking soda is used in a batter that is not acidic enough, there will not be enough carbon dioxide bubbles to make the batter rise. The baking soda that hasn't reacted with acid makes the batter taste very bitter.

How do you get your batter to rise if it doesn't contain much acid? You can use baking powder. Baking powder contains baking soda *plus* an acid. When baking powder is added to liquid ingredients, the baking soda in it reacts with the acid, and bubbles form. These bubbles expand in the oven, and the batter rises.

Some recipes call for both baking soda and baking powder. In these cases, there is probably some acid in the recipe but not enough to leaven the batter fully. Baking powder is needed in addition to baking soda to get the correct amount of leavening. After the batter is baked and removed from the oven, the carbon dioxide bubbles escape into the air. You are left with a delicately light cake, muffin, or biscuit. There should be no remaining bitter-tasting baking soda or baking powder.

B u t t e r m i l k   R a i s i n   M u f f i n s

1. Preheat the oven to 400°F (200°C).

2. Grease a muffin tin or place a paper liner in each muffin cup.

3. In a large bowl, mix thoroughly the flour, baking powder, cinnamon, baking soda, and salt.

4. In another bowl, mix together the buttermilk, egg, and oil.

5. Pour the wet ingredients into the dry ingredients and mix them only until the dry ingredients are moistened.

6. Stir in the raisins.

7. Spoon the batter into the prepared muffin tin.

8. Bake for 20 minutes, or until the muffins are slightly browned on the top and a toothpick inserted in the center of a muffin comes out clean.

9. Take the tin from the oven. Remove the muffins and let them cool on a wire rack. Serve warm or cool.

Makes 12 muffins.

2 cups flour

2 teaspoons baking powder

1 teaspoon cinnamon

1/2 teaspoon baking soda

1/2 teaspoon salt

1 cup buttermilk (the acid)

1 egg

1/4 cup vegetable oil

2/3 cup raisins

Why does cut fruit turn brown?

If you've ever bitten or cut into an apple, a pear, or a banana and then left it sitting around for a while, you've probably noticed that the fruit turns brown. Inside every fruit are pigment molecules that give it its color. When you cut open the fruit, these molecules are exposed to the air and start to turn brown.

Some kinds of fruit—apples, bananas, pears—turn brown more quickly than others—oranges, grapefruit, melons. That's because the first three have a special enzyme, a type of molecule that speeds up the browning. But this enzyme can be damaged, and the browning can be slowed down.

For example, if you cut apples and bake them in a pie, the oven's heat destroys the enzyme and stops the apples from turning brown. Or if you put sliced apples in the refrigerator, the cool temperature slows down the enzyme and the browning. Other ways to slow the enzyme—and the browning—include adding salt or acid to the fruit. Since highly salted fruit doesn't taste very good, most people add an acid such as lemon or orange juice to cut-up fruit to keep it looking fresh.

Summer Fruit Salad

1. In a large bowl, combine the peaches, pears, bananas, strawberries, and grapes.

2. Sprinkle the fruit with the orange juice.

3. Toss gently to mix well.

4. Sprinkle with coconut.

5. Refrigerate until ready to serve.

Makes 8 servings.

2 peaches, cut in bite-size pieces

2 pears, cut in bite-size pieces

2 bananas, sliced

1 cup strawberries, halved

1 cup grapes

1/4 cup orange juice

1/4 cup flaked coconut

If you want to make this fruit salad during a season when you can't find fresh peaches, use apples. If you can't find fresh strawberries, thaw frozen ones. Or combine your favorite fruits, keeping the total amount of fruit about equal to that in the recipe.

Why are pickles sour?

Pickles are cucumbers that have been treated so they can be eaten long after they are picked. There are sour pickles, and there are sweet pickles. But even sweet pickles are not entirely sweet—they're sweet and sour. There's a good reason why pickles are sour—they *need* to be. Why?

Almost all the food that you eat is also food for tiny living things called microbes that you can see only under a microscope. These microbes include bacteria, yeast, and molds. In most cases, they cause food to rot, making it taste bad. In some cases, such as cheese and yogurt, special microbes added to the food make the food what it is and give it its special taste.

Pickling: When you add an acid such as vinegar or lemon juice to vegetables, the acid kills the microbes and allows you to store the vegetables for a longer time without spoiling. The acid gives the food a sour taste.

Freezing: When you freeze food, you slow down the growth of microbes so much that the food does not spoil as quickly.

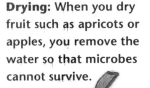

Drying: When you dry fruit such as apricots or apples, you remove the water so that microbes cannot survive.

SALT

Most microbes are fairly delicate and cannot live in places without enough water or where there is a lot of acid, sugar, heat, or cold. You can, therefore, slow down the growth of microbes by changing their environment.

Preserving, drying, salting, canning, freezing, and pickling are methods that allow us to enjoy all winter long the foods that we grow during the summer.

Canning: When you can fruits and vegetables, you heat them to a high temperature in the can to kill any unwanted microbes that would cause the produce to spoil.

Preserving: When you make jam, you add a large amount of sugar to the fruit. This draws water out of the microbes and kills them.

MICROBES BEWARE!

HELP!

Salting: When you make beef jerky, you add so much salt to the meat that water is drawn out of it. The microbes cannot live because water is no longer available.

Pickles are made by adding a mixture of vinegar, salt, sugar, and spices to cucumbers. You can also pickle other vegetables, such as green tomatoes, onions, peppers, mushrooms, and cauliflower. Here is a quick pickle recipe that's actually more like a Swedish cucumber salad than the pickles you get from a jar that require long pickling.

Puckered Pickles

1. In a large bowl or plastic container with a watertight lid, mix the vinegar, water, sugar, dill, and salt until the sugar and salt dissolve.

2. Add the cucumbers and onion. Mix well. Add pepper, if you like.

3. Cover the mixture and refrigerate it for at least 2 hours, stirring occasionally. (If the mixture is in a plastic container, turn the container over occasionally to mix the ingredients.)

Makes 6 to 8 servings.

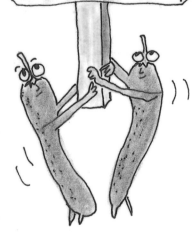

1/2 cup cider vinegar

1/2 cup water

1/4 cup sugar

1 tablespoon finely chopped fresh dill or 1 1/2 teaspoons dried dill weed

1 teaspoon salt

2 cucumbers, peeled and sliced thin

1 small red onion, peeled and sliced thin

Pepper to taste

SUGARS AND STARCHES

Do you have a sweet tooth? Most people do. It has been passed down, generation to generation, since prehistoric times. Before people grew their own food, their ability to taste sweetness helped them tell whether a plant was good or bad. Most plants that taste sweet are ripe and nutritious. Unripe and poisonous plants are usually bitter. Although we no longer need a sweet tooth to tell the difference between good and bad food, we are left with our love for sugar.

Plants make sugar through photosynthesis—a process by which they capture the energy from sunlight. They produce sugar to store energy and to build new plant cells. Plants store sugar in the form of starch, which is a long chain of sugar molecules. Seeds, such as corn kernels and rice, contain a lot of starch. The starch serves as the fuel that the seeds use for sprouting. Sugar molecules in plants can also form cellulose, which makes up the firm structure that holds plants together.

You use many different sugars and starches when you cook. In the following sections you will see how:

- *You can use concentrated sugar solutions to make candy.*

- *Starch thickens a sauce.*

- *The starch inside corn kernels explodes to make popcorn.*

How do you make candy from sugar?

Hard candy is made from sugar—the same granulated sugar that's in your sugar bowl. But how do you get hard, colored, glossy, solid candy from tiny white grains?

To make lollipops, for example, you need a syrup that is almost all sugar with just a tiny bit of water—1 to 2 percent—to keep it liquid. To make such a solution, mix the sugar and water together in a heavy pot until all the sugar dissolves. Then you boil away almost all the water.

How do you know when you reach 98 or 99 percent sugar? There are two ways to tell. One is by looking at the boiling temperature, as measured on a candy thermometer. The higher the sugar concentration, the higher the boiling temperature. The other method is by observing what happens when a small amount of the mixture is placed in ice water.

Temperature °F (°C)	Percent Sugar	Test Results
230 (110)	70%	Spins thread when dropped into ice water.
240 (116)	80%	Forms soft ball when dropped into ice water.
255 (124)	90%	Forms hard ball when dropped into ice water.
300 (149)	98-99%	Forms hard ball that cracks when dropped into ice water.

From the chart you can see that your lollipop mixture is ready when a small amount of it reaches 300°F (149°C) on the candy thermometer or forms a hard ball in the ice water.

36

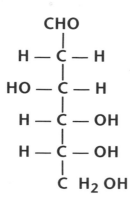

CHO
|
H — C — H
|
HO — C — H
|
H — C — OH
|
H — C — OH
|
C H$_2$ OH

C is a carbon atom.
H is a hydrogen atom.
O is an oxygen atom.

Sugar molecule

If you boil away a lot of the water and then cool the solution, it becomes supersaturated. This means it has more sugar in it than can stay in solution. Crystals of table sugar begin to form. Some candy, such as fudge, gets its texture from the formation of many tiny crystals. Rock candy forms when large crystals grow slowly. When making lollipops, you want to avoid crystallization, which gives lollipops a grainy texture.

There are two ways to avoid crystallization. One is to cool the mixture very quickly, so there is less time for the crystals to form. A second way is to add corn syrup to the table-sugar solution. Corn syrup is made of several different types of sugar molecules, with different shapes. They prevent the molecules of table sugar from stacking together into crystals.

In the lollipop recipe that follows, you will be doubly insured against crystallization by mixing corn syrup into your solution *and* by spooning the mixture into small portions, allowing the lollipops to cool quickly.

Loony Lollipops

Caution: Be extremely careful when working with hot sugar solution. It's even hotter than boiling water.

1/2 cup light corn syrup

1/2 cup water

1 cup sugar

1 teaspoon vanilla

4 drops red food coloring

Lollipop sticks, or wooden skewers cut in half

1. Line 3 baking sheets with aluminum foil. Place the lollipop sticks or wooden skewer halves on foil, about 3 inches apart.

2. In a 1-quart saucepan, mix the corn syrup, water, and sugar. Cook over high heat, stirring with a wooden spoon, until the mixture comes to a full boil. If sugar crystals form on the sides of the pan, wash them down with a pastry brush that has been dipped in water.

3. Boil the mixture until a candy/deep-fry thermometer registers 300°F (149°C), or until a small amount of syrup placed in a cup of ice water forms a hard ball that cracks.

4. Remove the pan from the heat. Stir in the vanilla and the food coloring. The vanilla will bubble when added to the hot syrup.

5. Carefully spoon the very hot mixture onto the lollipop sticks, making sure that the syrup covers the top inch or two of the stick.

6. The lollipops will be cool in about 20 minutes. Carefully peel them from the foil by gently lifting the sticks.

Makes about 24 two-inch lollipops.

What makes pudding and gravy lumpy?

Have you ever had a delicious turkey dinner with cranberries and sweet potatoes—and gravy with horrible little lumps in it? Gravies, sauces, and puddings get lumpy because their ingredients—starch, fat, and water—are added in the wrong order. The starch is what makes them thick, and it is also what causes lumps if used incorrectly. The most common starches used in cooking are cornstarch, potato starch, wheat flour, rice flour, tapioca, and arrowroot.

If you are making gravy, it is important to add the starch, usually wheat flour, to hot fat drippings or cool liquid. That way the bits of starch, called granules, get mixed evenly through the drippings. They can't clump together when added to the rest of the liquid.

Pudding can also get lumpy. Maybe you always eat pudding from plastic containers or from a mix. Then you may never have seen lumpy pudding. But when it is made from separate ingredients, it can turn out thin and lumpy. How does this happen? How can you prevent it?

If you add dry starch directly to hot water or milk (milk is mostly water), the starch granules become sticky on the outside and stay dry on the inside. The sticky granules lump together. These lumps, with raw starch on the inside, don't ever break up. They look strange and taste strange. And the rest of the pudding is thin.

Starch granules

Starch lump

But if you add starch to cold liquid, the individual starch granules are evenly dispersed, absorb the liquid, and swell like sponges. They don't get a chance to get lumpy. As you heat the mixture, even more liquid gets absorbed, and the pudding gets thicker.

As the pudding cools, starch molecules that have leaked out of the starch granules create a large net that keeps the liquid in the pudding from moving around. Your pudding then becomes thick and creamy.

OH, NO!

Oups!

1 square (1 ounce) unsweetened chocolate

2 cups milk (1 3/4 cups plus 1/4 cup)

1/2 cup sugar

1/8 teaspoon salt

2 tablespoons cornstarch

1/2 teaspoon almond extract

C h o c o l a t e - A l m o n d   P u d d i n g

1. In a 2-quart saucepan, combine the chocolate, 1 3/4 cups of the milk, the sugar, and the salt.

2. Cook and stir over medium heat until the milk is very hot but not boiling. The chocolate will not be completely melted.

3. In a small bowl, mix the cornstarch and the remaining 1/4 cup of milk until the cornstarch is completely dissolved.

4. Stir the cornstarch mixture into the hot milk. Cook over low heat, stirring constantly, until the mixture comes to a boil.

5. Boil and stir for 1 minute. (The chocolate should be completely melted.)

6. Remove from heat. Stir in the almond extract.

7. Pour the pudding into 4 individual custard cups or into a serving bowl.

8. Refrigerate for several hours, until the pudding sets.

Makes 4 servings.

Note: If you prefer, use 1 teaspoon vanilla instead of the almond extract.

Why does popcorn pop?

Can you think of any other food that changes as quickly as popcorn when it is cooked? Popcorn starts out as small, hard, golden kernels. In a split second it turns into light, fluffy, white or yellow puffs. How does that happen?

Corn contains water, protein, and starch. But not all corn pops, as Native Americans living at least 5,000 years ago discovered. That's because different types of corn contain different amounts of water, protein, and starch. They are used for different purposes, such as popcorn, corn oil, corn flour, for animal feed, and so on.

The corn used to make popcorn normally contains about 16 percent water when fresh. In order to make it pop, it is dried so that it contains between 13 and 14 percent water. After the popcorn has been dried, it is sealed in airtight containers to prevent the corn from absorbing water.

When you make popcorn, you must heat the kernels to a very high temperature in hot oil or by surrounding them with hot air in an air popper or a fireplace. Both oil and air can be heated to temperatures much higher than boiling water, which turns to steam at 212°F (100°C).

Popcorn kernel

Popcorn kernel with water heating inside

Popcorn kernel popped

As the temperature rises, the hot water inside the popcorn kernels starts to boil and turn into a gas (steam, or water vapor). If the kernels had small holes in them, the water vapor would be able to leak out. The casing of corn kernels is very hard, however, and does not allow the gas to escape. As the amount of trapped gas grows, the pressure inside the kernels increases. The hot kernels are like balloons that have been blown up all the way.

The pressure finally rises so high that the casings break and the popcorn kernels burst open just like popped balloons. Out fly all the starch, protein, and water vapor that were inside. The water vapor escapes quickly into the air and leaves behind the dry, fluffy puffs of starch and protein.

POP!

POP!

WEEEEEE!

POP!

POP!

POP!

POP!

POW!

POP!

PO

Freshly made popcorn left in a covered pot will quickly reabsorb the water vapor and become soggy. So it's important to pour freshly made popcorn into an open bowl and eat it!

Popcorn Nachos

1. Follow the manufacturer's directions for packaged popping corn, and go on to step 4, or follow steps 2 and 3.

2. In a 3-quart saucepan heat the oil. Add 2 or 3 of the popcorn kernels. When the kernels pop, add the remaining kernels and cover the pot.

3. Cook over medium heat, shaking the pan often. The popcorn will soon begin to pop. When the popping stops, remove the pan from the heat.

4. Quickly pour the popcorn into a shallow ovenproof serving dish or a baking sheet.

5. Sprinkle the popcorn with the grated cheese, then the chilies, and finally the chili powder.

6. Set the oven to broil (550°F, 288°C).

7. Broil the nachos for 2 to 3 minutes, until the cheese is melted. Serve immediately.

Makes 4 servings.

2 tablespoons vegetable oil

1/4 cup popcorn kernels

1 cup grated cheese

2 tablespoons diced mild green chilies

1 teaspoon chili powder

Popcorn Nachos can also be prepared in the microwave oven. Pour the popped corn into a shallow microwave dish. Assemble as above. Place the dish in the microwave oven and cook on high for 30 to 40 seconds, until the cheese is melted.

PROTEINS

Proteins are a type of molecule found in all animals and plants. Each protein is made from smaller molecules called amino acids. When you eat proteins, your body breaks them apart into amino acids and uses those amino acids to build new proteins that it needs.

In order for amino acids to form a protein, they link together into a long chain, like a line of people holding hands. There are only twenty different amino acids. They are all similar in shape, but each one contains its own unique side chain. It is as though each of the people in the line were wearing one of twenty different hats. An almost endless number of proteins can be formed by making chains of different lengths, each with a different combination of amino acids.

Every protein folds naturally into its own special shape. Some proteins are shaped like springs. Some are shaped like doughnuts. Some look like flat sheets. And some look like tangled balls of yarn. The shape of the protein determines what the protein does inside the plant or animal.

Proteins change dramatically when they are cooked. When proteins come in contact with heat, salt, alcohol, or an acid such as lemon juice, they start to unfold. Once they have lost their natural, folded shape, they are called denatured (unnatural) proteins.

Proteins are found in many foods you eat. Many of these foods are cooked specifically to change the proteins. In the sections that follow, you will see:

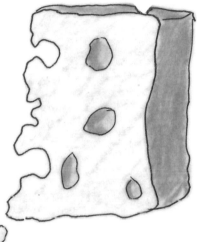

- *What happens to egg proteins when they are denatured.*

- *Why milk proteins curdle.*

- *How a protein called collagen is used to make gelatin.*

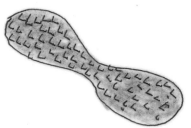

Why are hard-boiled eggs hard?

When you boil a liquid, what happens? More than likely it turns into a gas. If you boil it long enough, all the liquid boils away. But raw eggs are a liquid. When you boil them, they become solid! And once solid, they can never turn to liquid again. Why are eggs the exception to the rule?

Eggs are made of proteins, fats, and water. Most of an egg's proteins are shaped like tangled balls of yarn, and are called globular proteins. A raw egg is liquid because the water inside it is able to flow freely between the globular proteins.

When an egg is heated, all the molecules inside it begin to shake. The shaking causes the globular proteins to unwind. They are now in a denatured (unnatural) state. As they unwind, the denatured proteins get tangled with each other.

The water in both the white and the yolk gets trapped in the tangled net of denatured proteins. The egg becomes hard because the water can no longer move around freely.

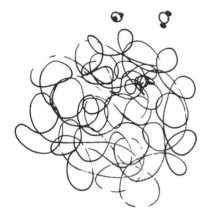

Whole proteins

When making scrambled eggs, if you add milk or water, it also becomes trapped in the protein net. The more the eggs are heated, the more the proteins unwind and become tangled, and the tighter the net becomes. If you overcook the eggs, the net becomes so tight that it starts to squeeze out the water in the milk. You end up with runny eggs.

When making poached eggs, where the raw eggs are cracked and placed gently on the surface of boiling water, most people add vinegar to the water. The vinegar helps denature the proteins on the surface of the eggs and prevents them from falling apart in the hot water before they are cooked through.

When making hard-boiled eggs, you can add salt to the water in order to prevent any egg white from leaking out of a crack in the shell. The salt will denature the leaking proteins even more quickly than the heat of the water, sealing the crack.

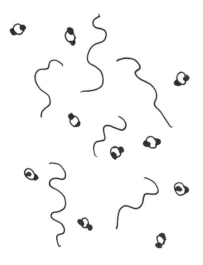

Denatured proteins

46

Dandy Deviled Eggs

1. Place the eggs in a medium saucepan with enough cold water to cover the eggs. Add 1 tablespoon salt. Heat until the water comes to a boil.

2. Turn down the heat so that the water is just simmering. Simmer the eggs for 10 minutes.

3. Pour off the hot water into the sink and fill the saucepan with cold water. Leave the eggs in the cold water until they are cool enough to handle.

4. Peel the shells off the eggs and cut the eggs in half the long way. Carefully scoop the egg yolks out into a small bowl. Place the whites on a serving plate and set it aside.

5. Mash the cooked yolks with a fork and stir in the mayonnaise and mustard. Add salt and pepper to taste. Mix until well blended.

6. Gently spoon the yolk mixture back into the egg-white halves. Garnish with chopped olives, parsley, dill, and/or paprika, if desired.

7. Refrigerate until ready to serve.

Makes 6 servings

6 eggs

Water

Salt

3 tablespoons mayonnaise

1 teaspoon Dijon-style mustard

Black pepper, to taste

[Finely chopped black olives, chopped fresh parsley, chopped fresh dill, or paprika, optional]

What are curds and whey?

In the Mother Goose rhyme, Little Miss Muffet sat on a tuffet, eating her curds and whey. But what *are* curds and whey? Actually, they are very common. They come from milk.

To understand how to make curds and whey, you need to understand the composition of milk. Milk is made up of several things, including fat, water, sugar, protein, and minerals.

The fat in milk is found in small, lumpy globules that float in the water. If you allow milk that's fresh from the cow to stand for a while, the fat globules float to the top and form a layer of cream. That's because the fat is lighter than water.

Most milk that we drink today is homogenized. This means that fresh milk is pumped through a valve at very high pressure to break the fat globules into very tiny balls. The tiny fat balls cannot rise as easily as the larger globules. They do not float to the top. Milk is also pasteurized—heated briefly to a high temperature. The heat kills microbes (germs), making the milk safe to drink and extending its shelf life (amount of time you can store it).

There are two groups of protein in milk, casein (kay-SEEN) and whey. Casein proteins exist naturally in small clusters that gently pull away from each other. These clusters are like tiny sponges that contain large amounts of water.

WHAT'D I DO?

When milk is heated or mixed with salt or acids (such as lemon juice), the denatured casein proteins no longer repel each other. Instead, they clump together and form solid curds. The remaining liquid is called the whey. Curds are mostly protein and fat, while whey is mostly water. If the entire mixture is squeezed through a cheesecloth, the curds that remain in the cloth can be used to make cheese.

Back in Miss Muffet's day, most cheese was made at home. Families made a lot of cheese at a time, because aged cheese can be stored and eaten over many months. The fresh curds and whey Miss Muffet was eating were a special treat eaten at cheese-making time.

You can enjoy fresh cheese, such as cottage cheese or ricotta, anytime. It requires just one step beyond making curds and whey and is very easy.

Ricotta Cheese

1 quart whole or low-fat milk

4 1/2 teaspoons white vinegar

Cheesecloth

1/8 teaspoon salt, or to taste

1. In a medium saucepan, mix the milk and the vinegar.

2. Place the pan over low heat and very slowly bring the mixture to a simmer. The milk will look slightly foamy, and there will be tiny bubbles around the edge.

3. Remove the pan from the heat. Cover it and set it in an enclosed place where it will not be disturbed and where its temperature will stay between 80°F and 100°F (27°-38°C). An unheated oven without a pilot light is fine. Let the milk stand about 6 hours, or until the curds and whey have separated.

4. Line a sieve with a double layer of cheesecloth and set it over a bowl or a 4-cup measuring cup it fits completely into.

5. Pour the curds and whey into the sieve and allow the whey to drain through the cloth and sieve for 1 hour.

6. Turn the cheese out of the cheesecloth into a small bowl. Stir in the salt. Cover and refrigerate 24 hours before serving.

Makes about 3/4 cup.

YOU CAN USE THIS CHEESE WHEN MAKING LASAGNA —OR YOU CAN EAT IT PLAIN.

50

What is gelatin?

A tiny amount of dry gelatin can turn a large bowl of liquid into a dessert that's wiggly, wet, and weird. Gelatin can also be used to thicken such foods as pies and marshmallows. What is gelatin and how does it work?

Gelatin is made from a unique protein called collagen that is found in your body and the bodies of most animals. Collagen is made of three separate chains of amino acids, the building blocks of proteins. The chains are like strands of rope twisted together. The three amino acid chains are held together by weak bonds. But overall, the collagen is very strong and forms the connective tissue that holds our bodies together.

When making gelatin, a manufacturer heats animal collagen to a very high temperature. Most of the weak bonds between the amino acid chains break. The denatured protein that results is then known as gelatin. You can make your own gelatin from meat bones by boiling some that have connective tissue on them. If you cool the broth you have made from them in a refrigerator overnight, it will not be liquid. It will be a gel.

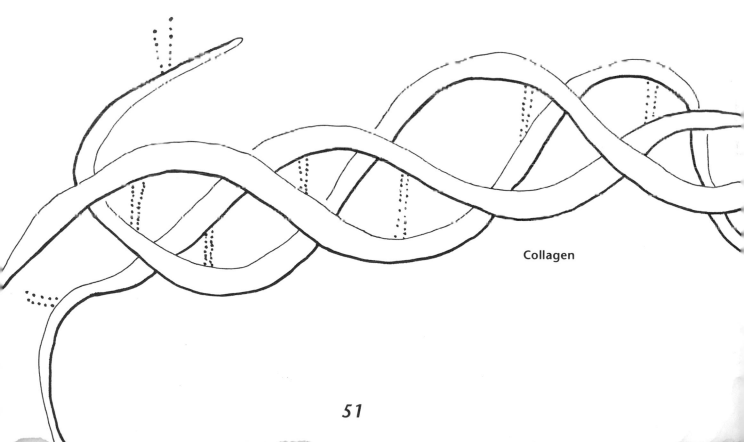

Collagen

When you use dry packaged gelatin in cooking, you add it to cold water. The cold water softens and spreads out the gelatin so that it does not clump together. Next, you heat the gelatin and water to dissolve the gelatin. After the gelatin is dissolved, you add the other ingredients. Then you refrigerate the whole mixture.

As the gelatin cools, the long amino acid chains form weak bonds again. But because the gelatin is mixed with other ingredients, it does not form the original bonds. It forms a big net that traps the liquid in the mixture. The more the gelatin cools, the more those bonds form and the more solid the mixture becomes.

Even in small amounts, gelatin is extremely good at turning liquids into solids. You can see how it works by making the marshmallows in the following recipe.

Is a gel a solid or a liquid? It is actually both. A gel contains a liquid trapped in a solid. That is what makes it wiggly.

Fresh pineapple contains an enzyme called bromelain that chops collagen into tiny pieces. So if you use fresh pineapple in gelatin, it won't gel. In canned pineapple the bromelain has been destroyed and won't hurt your gelatin.

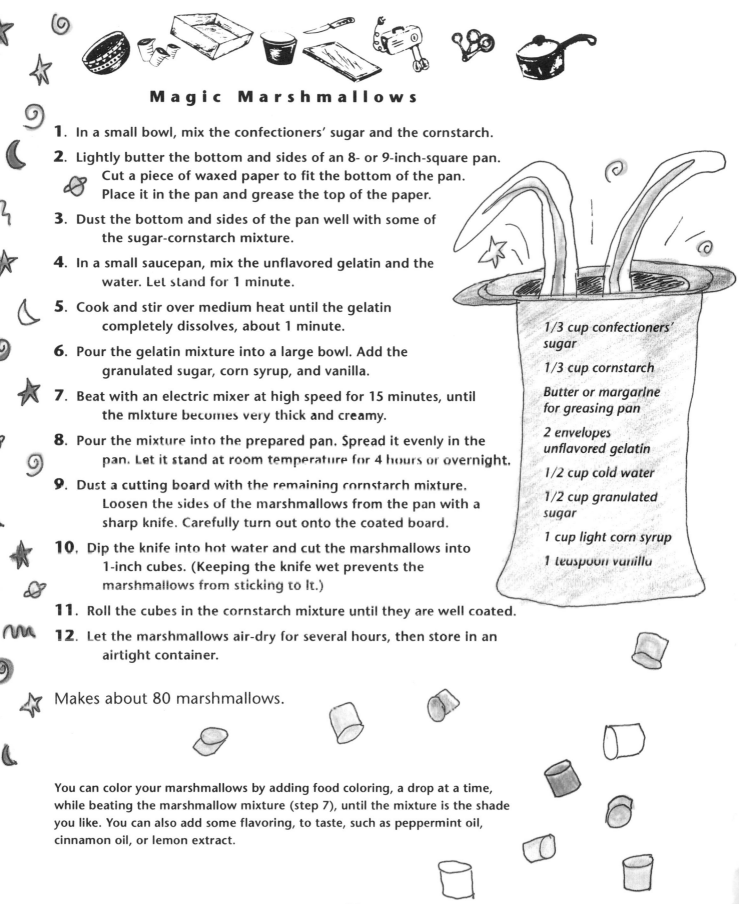

Magic Marshmallows

1. In a small bowl, mix the confectioners' sugar and the cornstarch.

2. Lightly butter the bottom and sides of an 8- or 9-inch-square pan. Cut a piece of waxed paper to fit the bottom of the pan. Place it in the pan and grease the top of the paper.

3. Dust the bottom and sides of the pan well with some of the sugar-cornstarch mixture.

4. In a small saucepan, mix the unflavored gelatin and the water. Let stand for 1 minute.

5. Cook and stir over medium heat until the gelatin completely dissolves, about 1 minute.

6. Pour the gelatin mixture into a large bowl. Add the granulated sugar, corn syrup, and vanilla.

7. Beat with an electric mixer at high speed for 15 minutes, until the mixture becomes very thick and creamy.

8. Pour the mixture into the prepared pan. Spread it evenly in the pan. Let it stand at room temperature for 4 hours or overnight.

9. Dust a cutting board with the remaining cornstarch mixture. Loosen the sides of the marshmallows from the pan with a sharp knife. Carefully turn out onto the coated board.

10. Dip the knife into hot water and cut the marshmallows into 1-inch cubes. (Keeping the knife wet prevents the marshmallows from sticking to it.)

11. Roll the cubes in the cornstarch mixture until they are well coated.

12. Let the marshmallows air-dry for several hours, then store in an airtight container.

1/3 cup confectioners' sugar

1/3 cup cornstarch

Butter or margarine for greasing pan

2 envelopes unflavored gelatin

1/2 cup cold water

1/2 cup granulated sugar

1 cup light corn syrup

1 teaspoon vanilla

Makes about 80 marshmallows.

You can color your marshmallows by adding food coloring, a drop at a time, while beating the marshmallow mixture (step 7), until the mixture is the shade you like. You can also add some flavoring, to taste, such as peppermint oil, cinnamon oil, or lemon extract.

CELLS

All living things are made of cells, which you can see only through a microscope. Cells are like tiny factories, each of which is designed to perform a specific task. The shape and size of each cell is determined by the task it performs.

Animal cells are like tiny bubbles filled with salty water. They have many specialized parts. The outside skin of each cell, called the membrane, is made of two layers of fat molecules.

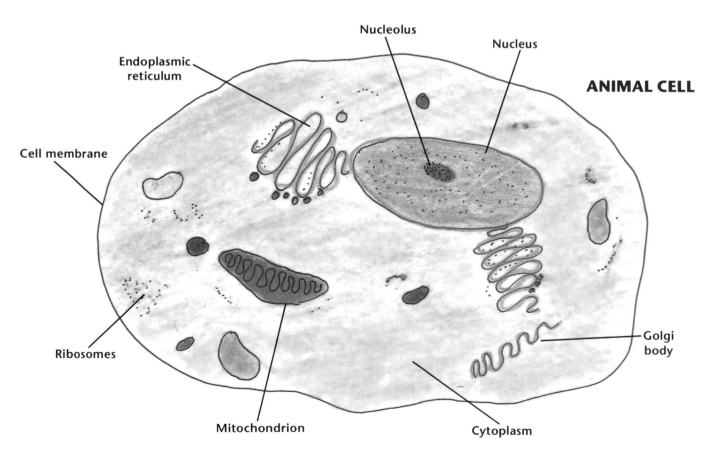

ANIMAL CELL

Nucleolus

Nucleus

Endoplasmic reticulum

Cell membrane

Ribosomes

Mitochondrion

Golgi body

Cytoplasm

54

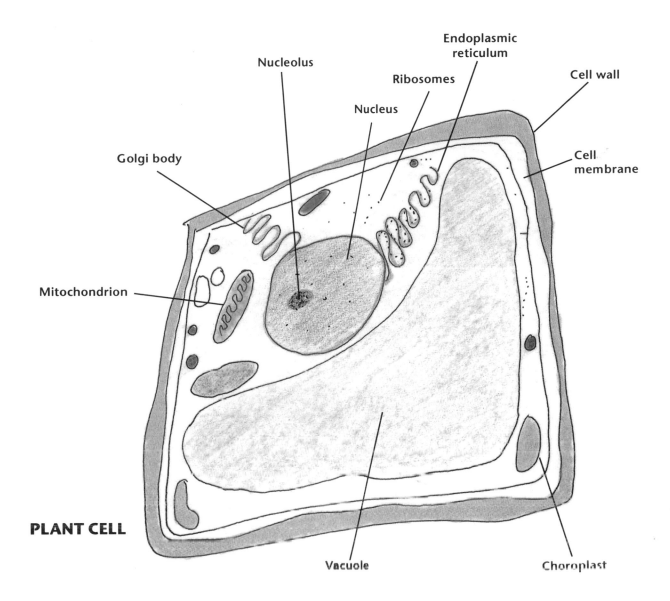

Nucleolus

Endoplasmic reticulum

Ribosomes

Nucleus

Cell wall

Golgi body

Cell membrane

Mitochondrion

PLANT CELL

Vacuole

Choroplast

Plant cells are somewhat different because they have an additional type of membrane around them, called a cell wall. The cell wall is much stronger than the cell membrane in animals. It helps plants withstand such forces of nature as strong winds and invading microbes. It gives some raw vegetables their crunch. In addition, a plant cell contains a large sac called a vacuole, which stores water.

Fungus cells are different from both plant and animal cells. Unlike plants, funguses do not make their own food. Funguses range from yeast, a single cell, to mushrooms.

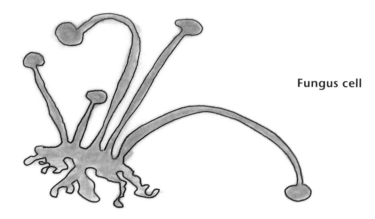

Fungus cell

Protists and monera also have only one cell. These tiny living things can be found in pond water, on your skin, in the food you eat—almost everywhere. But they are so tiny that you can see them only under a microscope.

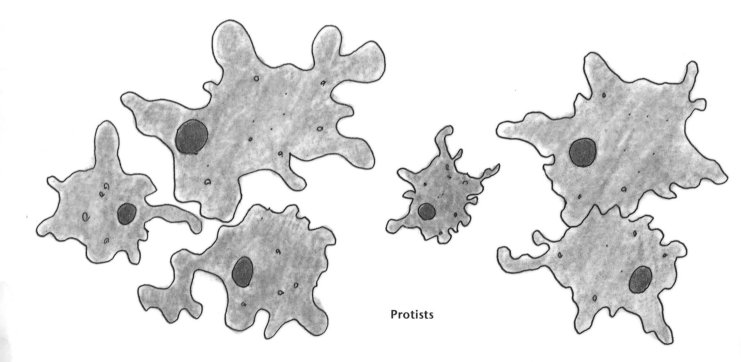

Protists

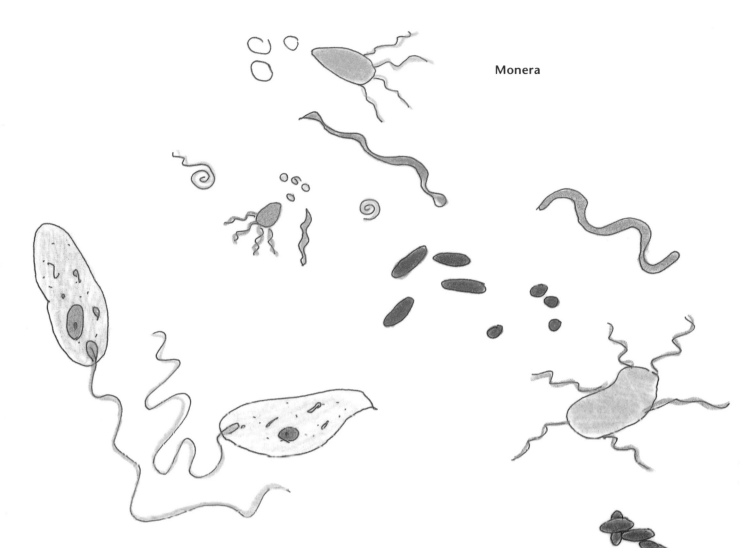

Monera

In the following sections, you will read about different types of cells. You will discover:

- *Why some plants wilt when they are cooked.*

- *How onions protect themselves from being eaten.*

- *How certain cells make bread rise.*

- *How cells create yogurt.*

- *How the light and the dark meat of a chicken differ, and why the differences are just as important to a chicken as to a cook.*

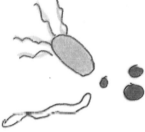

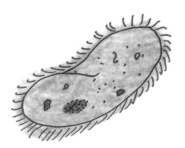

Why do some fruits and vegetables wilt when cooked?

Have you ever noticed that when you cook many fruits and vegetables, their texture changes from firm and crisp to limp and soft? Why does this happen?

The strong cell walls of a plant are made of cellulose, which forms the cell's framework. If the vacuole (sac) of each plant cell is filled with water, the plant is firm and rigid. When the sac is not full, the plant cells are limp and the leaves droop.

When you cook fruits and vegetables, the heat causes the cell walls to weaken, and the water to leak out of the cell. The plant becomes wilted and limp.

Some fruits and vegetables are more sensitive to heat than others. That depends on the strength of the cell walls, the amount of water in the cells, and the thickness of the plant part being used. Carrot (root) cells, for example, contain less water and have much stronger cell walls than do spinach (leaf) cells. As a result, carrots do not wilt as quickly as spinach when they are cooked. You can see the effect of heat on apples when you make the following recipe for apple crisp.

Q u i c k   A p p l e   C r i s p

1. Preheat the oven to 375°F (191°C).

2. In a large bowl, gently toss the apple slices, 1/4 cup of the packed brown sugar, and 1/4 teaspoon of the cinnamon. Pour into a greased 8-inch-square pan.

3. In a medium bowl, place the remaining 1/2 cup of sugar, the flour, the oatmeal, the butter, and the remaining 1/2 teaspoon of cinnamon. Mix them with your fingers until well blended.

4. Sprinkle the mixture over the apple slices. Bake for 30 minutes, or until the apples are tender and the topping is golden-brown.

5. Serve warm or cold. It is great with ice cream or whipped cream!

Makes 6 servings.

6 medium apples, peeled, cored, and sliced

3/4 cup packed brown sugar (1/4 cup plus 1/2 cup)

3/4 teaspoon cinnamon (1/4 teaspoon plus 1/2 teaspoon)

1/2 cup flour

1/2 cup uncooked oatmeal

1/3 cup butter or margarine, softened

Why do onions make you cry?

Have you ever cut an onion? How long does it take until your eyes start to burn and tears begin running down your face? If you never want onions to make you cry again, you can find out how it happens and how to prevent it.

Like other plants, onions are made up of cells. Onions cells have a special molecule that contains the chemical element sulfur. Between the cells is another molecule, called an enzyme, that speeds up chemical reactions. The sulfur-containing molecules and the enzymes sit quietly on opposite sides of cell wall—until the cells are cut open.

Then the sulfur-containing molecules and the enzymes come into contact and start a chain of chemical reactions. You cannot see these reactions, but you can feel the results. New molecules are released, float up into the air, and sting your eyes. Since the new molecules contain sulfur, when they react with the tears in your eyes, they form sulfuric acid. No wonder they burn!

CRYBABY!

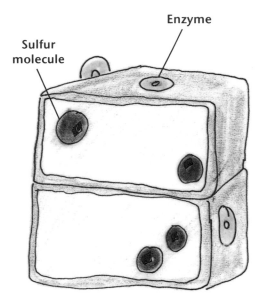

Sulfur molecule

Enzyme

Onion cells

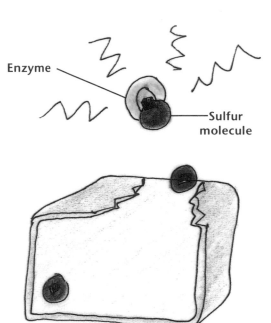

Enzyme

Sulfur molecule

Cut onion cell

The strong-smelling molecules in onions and garlic protect the plants from being eaten by small animals and bugs. People have learned to enjoy the flavor of these molecules in small amounts.

When you cook an onion, the molecules inside the onion cells are changed. They smell and taste much sweeter than raw onions too, and will not make you cry when they are cut.

Now that you know what causes onions to make you cry, there are things you can do to prevent it. As you cut an onion, you can put it under cold water. The burning molecules will react with the water before they get to your eyes. Or you can put the onion in the freezer 10 to 15 minutes before you cut it open. The reaction that takes place in the onion is slowed down by low temperatures, and fewer of the burning molecules will be formed.

When you prepare the onion soup that follows, which method will you choose to avoid having the onions make you cry?

French Onion Soup

3 large onions, sliced thin (about 4 cups)

4 tablespoons margarine or butter

3 cans (13 3/4 ounces each) beef broth

6 slices French bread, toasted

1 1/2 cups (6 ounces) shredded Swiss or Gruyère cheese

(You can use up to 12 ounces of cheese if you like.)

1. In a large pot over medium heat, cook onions in margarine, stirring occasionally, until onions are tender and start to brown.

2. Gradually stir in 1 can of the broth.

3. Heat to a boil, stirring constantly.

4. Stir in the rest of the broth and heat to a boil.

5. Reduce heat and simmer for 5 minutes.

6. Place 1 slice toast in each of 6 ovenproof soup bowls. (If you don't have these, you can finish preparing the soup in a large ovenproof casserole and spoon it into separate bowls after it is finished.)

7. Pour an equal amount of soup over toast in each bowl and sprinkle with equal amounts of cheese.

8. Set oven control to broil (550°F, 288°C).

9. Place tops of bowls 3-4 inches from heat and broil until cheese is melted and light brown, about 3 minutes. (If you have used more cheese, it will take a little longer.)

10. Be very careful when removing these very hot bowls from the oven. Use ovenproof mitts or pot holders. Let the soup cool off a bit so you don't burn your mouth when you eat it.

Makes 6 servings.

What is the difference between light and dark meat?

People eat the meat of many different animals, including chickens, cows, and fish. Most of the meat they eat comes from the animal's muscles. Some muscles are lighter in color and some are darker. Why?

If you look at different muscles under a microscope, you can see two types of muscle cells: white and red. Light meat has more white muscle cells. Dark meat has more red muscle cells.

Red muscle cells are designed to stay active for long periods of time. They are found in the legs of animals that run for long distances and in the wings of animals that fly for long periods of time. In order to maintain that activity, red muscle cells need energy. The source of the energy is fat, which is located in and around red muscle cells. In order to burn fat, these cells need oxygen. A special molecule called myoglobin stores oxygen in red muscle cells. It is bright red. This is why very active muscles are dark in color.

Myoglobin

Red muscle cells

White muscle cells

White muscle cells are found in muscles that are needed for only short bursts of activity, such as those in the breast and the wings of a chicken. These muscles can rely on the limited amount of sugar that circulates in the blood as a source of energy. As a result, these muscles do not have much fat. Since sugar can be burned without oxygen, these molecules do not have any need for myoglobin. These cells are light in color.

Fish have mostly white muscle cells. That's because fish float in the water and need only a small amount of energy to move around. Ducks, however, must work very hard for long periods of time when they are flying. As a result, the muscles in their wings and their breasts are composed mostly of red muscle cells.

Light meat and dark meat taste different from each other. Which one do you like best? Here's a recipe that can use either one—or both.

Thai Chicken Kabobs

1. In a medium bowl or plastic container with a watertight lid, blend the peanut butter, honey, soy sauce, water, ginger, and red pepper.

2. Add the chicken pieces and mix well. Cover and marinate in the refrigerator for at least 2 hours, stirring occasionally. (If the chicken is in a plastic container, turn the container over occasionally to mix ingredients.)

3. Preheat the oven to 425°F (218°C).

4. Cover a baking sheet with aluminum foil. Thread the chicken pieces onto the skewers, leaving spaces between the chicken pieces. Place the skewers on the baking sheet.

5. Bake 10 minutes. Turn the chicken skewers over and bake for 10 minutes longer, until the chicken is tender.

6. Remove from the oven and serve hot.

Makes 4 servings.

3 tablespoons creamy peanut butter

3 tablespoons honey

2 tablespoons soy sauce

1 tablespoon water

1/4 teaspoon ground ginger

Dash of ground red pepper (cayenne)

About 1 1/4 pounds boneless chicken breasts or thighs or a combination of both, cut into 1 1/2-inch squares

Wooden skewers

Why does yeast make bread rise?

There is something almost magical in the way bread rises. But it isn't really magic. It's yeast and gluten. What are they, and how do they make bread rise?

Yeast is a kind of microbe, a living thing that can be seen only under a microscope. It is made up of just one cell and belongs to the fungus family (which includes mushrooms). Yeast can be stored in an inactive state for long periods of time in packets in your refrigerator. When it is added to warm, moist bread dough, it comes back to life. The yeast eats the starch in the dough, which gives the yeast energy to reproduce.

While digesting the starch, yeast gives off carbon dioxide gas and alcohol as waste products. The alcohol evaporates into the air, and the carbon dioxide gas becomes trapped as bubbles in the dough. The gas bubbles are trapped because the dough contains gluten. Gluten is a tangled net of protein that is formed when water is added to flour. Gluten is stretchy, like bubble gum, and can contain the expanding gas. The more the dough is kneaded, the more gluten is formed.

As the yeast consumes the starch in the dough, it produces more and more carbon dioxide gas. The gas pockets expand, causing the dough to rise. You then "punch" down the dough to collapse many of the gas bubbles. If you let the dough rise too long, the yeast will be killed by the gas, its own waste. But the dough can be allowed to rise again and then punched down any number of times before it is shaped into a loaf. The number of risings changes the texture of the bread.

Traditional bread loaves are allowed to rise twice before they are put into a hot oven. Other risen products, such as pretzels and pizza dough, are put into the oven with only one rising. In the oven, the dough gets very hot, the yeast dies, and no more carbon dioxide gas is produced.

The gas *already* in the bread dough continues to expand—all gases expand when they are heated—and the loaf continues to grow.

When the outside of the loaf gets hard and crusty, and the loaf cannot expand anymore, the bread is done. It is then allowed to cool as the gas seeps into the air. It leaves behind the tiny holes you see when you look at a slice of bread.

The key to making yeast bread is to provide a comfortable place for the yeast to grow. It needs a wet, warm environment and plenty of food. Warm water provides the moisture, and sugars derived from the starch in the flour serve as the food. With these simple ingredients, yeast helps you to transform a lump of dough into homemade bread.

Baking your own yeast bread can be fun. Making your own pizza is another way to use yeast that's sure to be a crowd pleaser.

Pretty Perfect Pizza

1. In a large bowl, combine the water and the yeast. Let them stand for 5 minutes.

2. Stir in the oil and salt. With a wooden spoon, stir in the flour, a cup at a time, until the dough forms a ball that leaves the sides of the bowl.

3. Turn the dough out onto a floured surface and knead it for 8 to 10 minutes, adding flour as needed to prevent the dough from sticking to your hands and to the work surface. The dough is kneaded enough when it feels smooth and elastic. When you press it lightly with your finger, it should spring back, leaving only a slight dent.

4. Shape the dough into a smooth ball and place it in a lightly greased bowl, turning the dough until it is coated with oil. Cover the bowl with plastic wrap.

5. Let the dough rise in a warm, draft-free place for about 1 hour, until it has doubled in size.

1 cup warm water (about 105°F to 115°F, 41°C to 46°C—water should feel comfortably warm when sprinkled on the inside of your wrist)

1 envelope active dry yeast

2 tablespoons vegetable oil

1 teaspoon salt

About 3 cups flour

2/3 cup pizza or spaghetti sauce

1 1/3 cups shredded mozzarella cheese

[Sliced mushrooms, green pepper, pepperoni, etc., optional]

6. Punch down the dough with your fist. Knead it for a minute or two until it is very smooth. Let the dough rest for 5 minutes.

7. Preheat the oven to 450°F (232°C).

8. Lightly grease a 12-inch pizza pan or a 13 X 9 X 2-inch baking pan.

9. Roll out the dough with a rolling pin into as large a circle as possible. Then stretch the dough with your fingers until it fits the pan.

10. Spread the sauce over the surface of the dough. Bake on the lower oven shelf for 25 minutes.

11. Remove the pan from the oven and cover the sauce with the cheese. Top with mushrooms, green peppers, or whatever you like on your pizza. Return the pizza to the oven and bake 10 minutes longer, until the cheese is melted.

Makes one pizza.

How to knead dough

Sprinkle a little of the flour from the recipe on a clean work surface. Rub a little flour on your hands. Turn the dough out onto the floured surface. Fold it toward you with your fingers. Push the dough down with the heel of your hands. Give the dough a quarter turn, and repeat the fold and the push. Continue turning, folding, and pushing until the desired consistency is reached, adding flour to the work surface and your hands anytime the dough starts to stick.

What is yogurt?

Bacteria are one-celled microbes even tinier than yeast. When two types of bacteria—*Lactobacillus bulgaricus* and *Streptococcus thermophilus*—are added to milk, the texture and flavor of the milk changes. It becomes yogurt. How does this happen?

Like yeast, bacteria like to eat sugar. The kind of bacteria found in yogurt eat only lactose, a sugar naturally found in milk. When they eat the sugar, they release lactic acid, which makes the milk taste sour. Also, a substance called an aldehyde is formed, which gives yogurt its special flavor.

When the amount of acid in the milk gets high enough, the milk proteins clump together and form lumpy curds. (See the section on curds and whey for more information.) Since the enclosed whey cannot move around in the solution as much as it did in the fresh milk, yogurt is thicker than milk.

Lactobacillus bulgaricus

Streptococcus thermophilus

IT'S ALIVE!

Yogurt is very easy to make at home. All you need is milk and special lactic-acid bacteria. You can get the bacteria from store-bought yogurt that contains active cultures. (Check the manufacturer's label. Not all yogurt contains active bacteria.)

Temperature control is important to yogurt making. If the temperature gets too high, the bacteria will die. On the other hand, lowering the temperature too much, by placing the yogurt in the refrigerator, stops lactic-acid production altogether. (This is why you store yogurt there.) But if the yogurt is warmed, the bacteria will start reproducing again.

You can make yogurt in a commercial yogurt maker, in your oven, or even in a thermos!

The curds and whey in yogurt are very delicate and can separate if the yogurt is stirred too much or if it is heated to high temperatures. For example, if you stir a container of yogurt and then put it back into the refrigerator, a day later you will find that there is a watery layer on the top. This liquid is whey that has been squeezed out of the curds, just as water is squeezed out of a sponge. If you stir the yogurt to mix the curds and whey, the yogurt will be thinner than it was originally, but it will taste the same.

Although the first commercial yogurt company was founded in Spain in 1919, people have been eating yogurt for thousands of years in Asia and the Middle East. Goat's milk, sheep's milk, and yak's milk are used in various places. People in the mountains of Armenia and Georgia (formerly parts of the Soviet Union near Turkey) eat lots of yogurt.

Homemade Yogurt

2 cups whole or low-fat milk

2 tablespoons plain yogurt with active cultures

3 tablespoons nonfat dry milk

1. In a 1-quart saucepan, heat the milk until it is 100°F to 115°F (38°C to 46°C). (The milk will feel comfortably warm when sprinkled on the inside of your wrist.)

2. Stir in the yogurt and the dry milk until well blended.

3. Put the mixture in a warm place for 4 to 6 hours until the yogurt is thick. For this you can use a commercial yogurt maker (follow the manufacturer's instructions); place the pan in a 100°F (38°C) oven (see Note A); or pour the mixture into a prewarmed thermos (see Note B).

4. Refrigerate the yogurt for several hours. It will thicken as it cools.

5. Serve the yogurt plain, add fruit to it, or mix it with herbs to make a salad dressing.

Makes about 2 cups.

Note A: Since ovens don't have a temperature setting as low as 100°F (38°C), it is necessary to use an oven thermometer that registers as low as 100°F. Turn the oven on to the lowest setting. When the oven thermometer registers 100°F, turn the oven off. It may be necessary to repeat this procedure every hour or so. Do not let the oven temperature get higher than 115°F (46°C). You might kill the lactic-acid bacteria.

Note B: To prewarm the thermos container, fill it with boiling water. Let it stand a couple of minutes. Pour off the water. Then fill the thermos with the warm milk mixture. Cover and set it where it will not be disturbed. Rewarm the thermos in the sink every 2 to 3 hours by pouring boiling water around the outside of the thermos. Return it to its undisturbed place between warmings.

GLOSSARY

ACID See pH.

ALCOHOL In bread making, a waste product that yeast gives off.

AMINO ACID Any of the 20 basic building blocks of proteins. A chain of amino acids forms a protein.

ATMOSPHERIC PRESSURE The push downward on Earth and all objects on Earth by the weight of the air in the atmosphere.

ATOM The smallest particle of any chemical element that can exist either alone or together with other atoms.

BACTERIA Microscopic one-celled creatures that multiply very quickly. They live in air, soil, water, animals, plants, and remains of living things.

BASE See pH.

BOILING The change of a liquid to a gas at a specific temperature, which is called the boiling point.

BOND The strong attraction that holds together atoms in a molecule and molecules in a compound.

CARBOHYDRATE A group of molecules made of carbon, hydrogen, and oxygen, that includes sugars, starches, and cellulose.

CARBON DIOXIDE A colorless gas made of carbon and oxygen. Animals breathe out carbon dioxide and plants breathe it in.

CASEIN A kind of protein found in milk that clumps together when exposed to acid, salt, or high temperatures.

CELL The most basic unit of all living things able to function by itself.

CELLULOSE A long sugar molecule, similar to starch, that gives a plant cell a strong structure.

CELL WALL The strong cell membrane that surrounds individual plant cells.

CHEMICAL REACTION The way in which chemicals combine.

CHEMICAL RELATIONSHIP A permanent bond that exists between the atoms and molecules of different substances, such as when you mix salt and water.

COLLAGEN A very strong protein found in animals that is used to make gelatin.

COMPOUND A substance made up of more than one kind of atom. Examples include water, alcohol, fat, sugar, and starch.

CRYSTAL A solid in which the atoms line up in the same geometric pattern over and over again.

CURD The thick, lumpy part of milk that has been exposed to acid, heat, or high temperatures.

DENATURING The destruction of the original properties of a molecule.

ELEMENT One of about a hundred substances that consist of only one kind of atom and that by themselves or in combination make up all matter.

EMULSIFIER A substance that contains a "water-loving" molecule on one end and a "water-fearing" molecule on the other end. Its presence allows you to mix substances such as oil and water that you can't usually mix.

ENERGY The ability to do work. There are several forms of energy, including heat, electrical, and mechanical energy.

ENZYME A protein that speeds up a specific chemical reaction.

EVAPORATION The slow change of a liquid into a gas, such as water into vapor.

FAT A kind of molecule that is stored by animals and plants as an important source of energy.

FREEZING The change of a liquid to a solid at a specific temperature, the freezing point. This is the same temperature as the melting point.

GAS A state of matter in which the particles are far apart, move freely inside a container, and fill any space available.

GELATIN Collagen that has been denatured by boiling. Gelatin is used to create a gel, a solid with a liquid trapped inside.

GLOSSARY

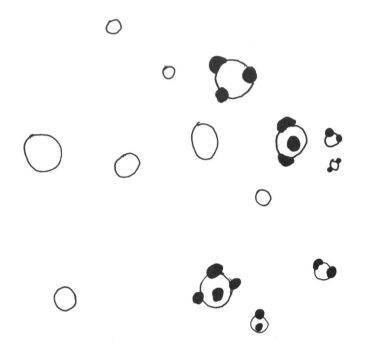

MICROBE A tiny living thing so small that it can be seen only under a microscope. Examples of microbes include bacteria and yeast.

MOLECULE The smallest particle of a substance that has the properties of that substance. A molecule is made up of atoms.

MYOGLOBIN A large protein found in red muscle cells that holds oxygen from the blood for later use by active muscles.

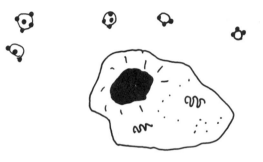

GLUTEN A rubbery mixture of wheat protein and water, formed when bread dough is kneaded. Gluten helps contain the carbon dioxide gas produced by yeast in bread making.

HOMOGENIZATION The process of creating a solution that is the same all over. Milk is homogenized by breaking the fat globules into tiny balls so they do not rise to the surface of the milk.

LIQUID A state of matter in which the volume of a substance stays the same but the shape depends on the shape of the container it is in.

MATTER Matter is something that has weight and takes up space. Matter exists in one of three states: solid, liquid, and gas.

MELTING The change of a solid into a liquid at a specific temperature, which is called the melting point. This is the same temperature as the freezing point.

NUCLEUS The part of animal and plant cells where instructions are given for cell functions and making new cells.

OIL A fat that is a liquid at room temperature.

PASTEURIZATION The process of heating a substance, such as milk, to a high temperature to kill unwanted microbes.

pH A measure of how acidic (sour) or basic (bitter) a solution is. A pH equal to 7.0 is neutral (neither acidic nor basic). A pH below 7.0 is an acid, and a pH above 7.0 is a base.

PIGMENT A type of molecule that gives color to a substance.

PROTEIN One of the most common kinds of molecules in living things. They are made up of one or more chains of amino acids.

RED MUSCLE CELLS Muscle cells found mainly in the legs and wings of animals that run and fly long distances. These cells can be active for long periods of time.

SOLID A substance that has a definite shape.

SOLUTION A mixture in which one or more ingredients dissolves in a liquid.

STARCH A long molecule made of a chain of sugar molecules bonded together.

SUGAR Any of a group of sweet-tasting carbohydrates.

VAPOR PRESSURE The upward pressure from liquid molecules that have turned to a gas. As the temperature rises (as in boiling) the vapor pressure increases.

WHEY The watery portion of milk that remains when the casein proteins are curdled by acid or salt.

WHITE MUSCLE CELLS Muscle cells that are very active for brief periods of time and use blood sugar as a source of energy.

YEAST A type of one-celled microbe used to help bread dough rise.

INDEX

There are several people I would like to thank for helping to make this book possible. First is my editor, Marc Gave, who expertly managed this project. Next is Lucy Holtzman Gave, who tested all of the recipes and made delicious suggestions. I would also like to acknowledge Dick Kleyn and Lucy Williams, for their technical comments on the manuscript, and Bo Park, for her comments based on teaching food chemistry to kids.

THE END

Using Dreamweaver®
To Create Software
Demonstrations

An e-Learning Developer's
Step-by-Step Guide to Creating
Native HTML Software Demos

1st Edition

Garin Hess and Steven Hancock

Rapid Intake Press
www.rapidintakepress.com

Using Dreamweaver® to Create Software Demonstrations: An e-Learning Developer's Step-by-Step Guide to Creating Native HTML Software Demos

ISBN: 0-9715080-2-X

Published by Rapid Intake Press, a division of Rapid Intake Inc.

Rapid Intake, Inc.
1014 SE 144th CT
Vancouver, WA 98683

(360) 882-7307
FAX (360) 896-6142
www.rapidintake.com

Printing History
September 2002: First Edition

Warning and Disclaimers
The authors and publisher of this book have made their best efforts in the preparation of this book and all the electronic examples to make them complete and as accurate as possible. The authors and publisher make no warranty, express or implied, on the information and programs in this book.

Trademarks
Numerous trademark names are used throughout this book. Every effort has been made to place indication marks on the first occurrence. The publisher cannot ensure the accuracy of this information. All trademark names have been used for the purpose of communicating the information in the book and for the benefit of the trademark owner with no intention of infringing upon that trademark.

http://www.rapidintake.com

Table of Contents

Introduction

If you are creating an e-learning course that teaches a software application, you may want to show the learner how to do a particular task using a demonstration. Demonstrations are an important instructional design principle, and you should consider a demonstration where time and expense allows it.

There are many tools you can use to create software demonstrations, and Dreamweaver may not be the best choice in every situation. However, Using Dreamweaver's tools you can create a software demonstration that is relatively simple to create and requires no plug-in because it uses HTML and JavaScript. Moreover, the file size of demos created in a native HTML environment can be surprisingly small when compared to other tools used to create demos.

This e-book gives you step-by-step instructions for creating these kinds of demonstrations using Dreamweaver

In this book you will learn how to:

- Use Dreamweaver timelines to control the sequence of the demonstration.
- Use HTML layers to create images that you can hide and show in the course of the demonstration.
- Use Dreamweaver behaviors to hide and show the appropriate elements of the demonstration at the correct times.
- Add JavaScript to your demonstration to mimic keyboard data entry.
- Use animated GIFs to illustrate mouse clicks.
- Incorporate demo annotations.
- Pre-load images so the demo runs smoothly once it starts.

Prerequisite Knowledge

To get the most out of this book you need to have a foundation in certain topics. You don't absolutely need these prerequisites, but they will be helpful.

Dreamweaver MX Fundamentals

To get the most out of this book, you should have a working knowledge of Dreamweaver MX. We will guide you through all of the necessary steps to create software demonstrations, but if you already have a foundation in Dreamweaver, you will find the instructions much easier to follow.

More Information: Read our book titled Fundamental e-Learning Techniques Using Dreamweaver MX for a solid foundation in Dreamweaver and e-learning development principles. You can find more details about this book at the Rapid Intake Press website (www.rapidintakepress.com).

JavaScript

While it is not necessary to know JavaScript to create software demonstrations, there are certain chapters where a basic knowledge of JavaScript will be helpful.

Screen Capture Utility

There are numerous screen capture utilities on the market. The one we prefer is called SnagIt®, published by TechSmith (see www.SnagIt.com). All of the exercises in this book already have the screen captures done for you. However, when you create your own software demonstrations you will need a good screen capture utility. We'll explain more about what features it should have later.

Which Version of Dreamweaver Does this Book Address?

This book focuses on using Dreamweaver MX. However, Dreamweaver 4 could also be used with very few differences.

Conventions Used in this Book

In this book we have used these conventions to make information more readily accessible.

Icons Used in the Book

There are seven icons used in the book. Each icon is explained here:

 Note: The note icon is placed beside a note that contains extra information or important information about the current topic.

 Caution: The exclamation point icon is placed beside a caution. Pay close attention to this information.

 Tip: The light-bulb icon is placed beside a tip. The tips in this manual are practical and very helpful.

 More Information: The books icon is placed beside a cross-reference. A cross-reference directs you to another place in the book or separate information altogether.

 On CD: The CD icon is placed next to information that is also contained on the companion CD. You can find more information about what the CD contains in the section What is on the CD ROM? later in this introduction.

 Hands-On: The hands-on icon is placed next to a section header. This icon indicates that the section contains step-by-step instructions and sample files on the CD ROM that lets you follow along. At the completion of a hands-on exercise, you will have created an interaction or made some change to an e-learning application.

Typographical Conventions

This book uses a few typographical conventions that you should be aware of:

- We reference menus using an arrow between each menu option. For example, Window → Common Libraries → Buttons refers to the menu option "Buttons" that is inside the submenu "Common Libraries" that is inside the menu "Window".

- Code font usually indicates JavaScript or HTML code. If a lengthy piece of code is included, we set it off in its own paragraph.

- We always number step-by-step procedures. This will make it easy for you to follow.

- The instructions in this book, work in both Macintosh and Windows environments. If there is a difference, we will indicate what that difference is for the Macintosh environment.

- We indicate keyboard keys by using small caps. (For example, press the ENTER key).

What are the Accompanying Files?

The accompanying files contain numerous examples used throughout the book. In the hands-on sections, you are instructed to open certain files to begin a step-by-step or to see the final results. You may want to copy the files to your hard drive before you begin using them.

Note: The sample files have been designed to work with Dreamweaver MX. For the best possible experience, use Dreamweaver MX. If you don't want to purchase a full version, download the 30-day trial from Macromedia at www.macromedia.com/dreamweaver.

Overview of Main Steps

Before we get started, let's take a look at the big picture. To create a software demonstration you need to know how to use these Dreamweaver tools:

- Layers
- Behaviors
- Timelines

The overarching steps behind creating a software demonstration in Dreamweaver are:

1 Take screen captures of all steps in the demonstration.

2 Place each of these screen captures in a layer and stack them according to the order they will appear in the demonstration.

3 Create a mouse image, place it in a layer, and set its Z-index to *999* so that it always appears on top of the other images.

4 Add the mouse image to a Dreamweaver timeline.

5 Animate the mouse using the timeline and at the appropriate positions, add **Show/Hide Layers** behaviors to the timeline to show the layers that contain the screenshots.

6   Either start the timeline automatically by choosing the *Autoplay* option on the timeline panel, or start the timeline based on another event by using the **Start Timeline** behavior.

7   (Optional) Use animated GIFs to illustrate mouse clicks.

8   (Optional) Use layers to annotate the demonstration with explanations and instructions.

You will follow these steps as you work through a comprehensive hands-on exercise in this book.

 On CD: Take time to explore two samples on the CD. Look at /sample_1/sw_demo_sample.htm for a simple example of a software demo. Open /sample_2/sample_2-8.htm on the companion CD to view a more complex example. You will be creating this demo as the main exercise in this book.

Creating Screen Captures 1

Before you start working in Dreamweaver, you need to take pictures of the software application so you can use them in the demonstration. These pictures are called *screen captures*.

In this chapter we'll provide some basic steps for creating screen captures using the screen capture utility SnagIt. Of course you can use the screen capture utility you feel most comfortable with, but we really like some of the features that SnagIt provides.

In this chapter you learn how to:

■   Use the SnagIt screen capture utility to take screen captures.

■   Establish SnagIt setting that will save you time creating the screen captures.

■   Organize your screen capture files for ease of maintenance.

Getting Started With SnagIt

SnagIt is a sophisticated utility, and it is not our purpose to explain every use of SnagIt. However, if you haven't used SnagIt before, you can use this section as guide for getting started quickly.

The two main settings are the *Input* and the *Output*. The *Input* setting allows you to choose what type of capture you are going to make. The *Output* setting determines what SnagIt does with the image once the capture is made.

Note: SnagIt is only compatible with Windows-based operating systems. For a list of some screen capture programs for the MAC, see http://allmacintosh.xs4all.nl/scaptmac.html. A screen capture utility that offers many of the same features as SnagIt is Snapz Pro. Snapz Pro is available for Mac OS 7-9 or Mac OS X. See http://www.ambrosiaSW.com/utilities/ for more information.

Input Options

Choosing the correct input setting can make a big difference in the final outcome of the software demonstration. Some of SnagIt's input settings also make your life easier. Here is a list of settings and their explanations. (All explanations in this table are taken directly from the SnagIt online help, used with permission from TechSmith Corporation.)

Setting	Explanation
Screen	Click the Screen option from the SnagIt Input menu to capture the full Windows desktop (everything seen on the screen).
Window	Select Input → Window to capture all of a user selected window or a part of it. The captured IMAGE can include the full window inside the border, title bar, menu bar, scroll bars or caption line.

Setting	Explanation
Active Window	Select Input → Active Window to capture the active window (the window that has the focus on the Windows desktop when SnagIt is started).
Region	Select Input → Region to capture a rectangular region of the screen you select.
Fixed Region	Select Input → Fixed Region to capture a rectangular fixed region of the screen. The dimensions and location can be typed in screen pixel coordinates.
Object	Use Object Capture to capture small items on your computer screen. Select Input → Object to capture Windows objects. This can give you better control over exactly what is captured, depending on your goal. For example, use Object input with Image Capture, to capture icons from toolbars. And in Text Capture mode, the Object Name, Description, and Value can be captured.
Menu	This input option is helpful for capturing drop-down menus from windows programs with the cursor in the IMAGE.
Shapes	The Shape capture menu allows you to select from one of five different shapes on screen to be captured. Start capture by clicking the mouse and dragging an area. After starting the capture, the cursor changes to a crosshair pointer to let you outline the capture area. During capture, a small preview window shows the X and Y coordinates, the Height and Width, and the vicinity being captured.

There are also some advanced input options that we do not attempt to explain here.

Output Options

Choosing the correct output can save you a lot of time too. SnagIt has some output settings that allow you to take successive screen captures that are automatically turned into image files in a directory of your choosing and numbered sequentially.

Here is a list of settings and their explanations: (All explanations in this table are taken directly from the SnagIt online help, used with permission from TechSmith Corporation.)

Setting	Explanation
Printer	Select Output → Printer to send the captured IMAGE or TEXT to a printer. The status display shows the Output option is set to Printer and a check mark is adjacent to the option.
Clipboard	Select Output → Clipboard to send the captured IMAGE or TEXT to the Windows clipboard. When an IMAGE or TEXT is on the clipboard, it can be put in a different Windows Program or saved as a clipboard file (.CLP) or as an ASCII text file (.TXT).
File	The Output → File option changes depending on the type of capture you are performing. For all types of capture, you are offered file naming and folder options. SnagIt can be set to ask for a file name, allow you to give a fixed file name and folder, or automatically name files.
Send Mail	Use this option to send captured IMAGE files and optional short messages to e-mail recipients.
Catalog	When storing new image captures to the SnagIt Catalog Folder, the default image file type is set using the Output → Properties… → Image File tab dialog. That is, the file type for new image files added to the Catalog is the current SnagIt Output image file type.

Setting	Explanation
Web	Use Web Output to send captured output to a web server. Set up SnagIt for timed or regular capture and specify the necessary data on the Output Properties Dialog Web tab. This allows you to send anything you have captured from your computer to the web site for automatic loading using SnagIt's FTP interface features. Using image capture, for example, SnagIt can send a still image to an FTP server each 20 seconds (using Timed Capture), overwriting the image each time it is sent. The web page can be set to automatically refresh in the user's browser when the image is renewed, always showing a new image.
Studio	Output → Studio sends images you capture to SnagIt Studio as the background image to annotate and enhance.
Preview Window	Select Output → Preview Window to be able to preview captured files before output. This is useful when selecting SnagIt color, print and content options that otherwise make repetitive and time consuming printed output necessary. After seeing the preview, continue creating the output, cancel the current capture or redirect the capture to the printer or file. When Preview Window is selected, captured files open in a viewing window before being output. Because the Preview Window is a disconnected window, other tasks can be done with it open. Changes can be made in your SnagIt configuration; a new capture can be started and then previewed without closing the Preview Window.
Multiple Outputs	SnagIt allows users to send output only to one destination at a time unless you select multiple output. Use Output → Multiple Outputs to send captures to more than one destination at a time (a file and the printer, for example).

Creating Your First Capture

Once you've chosen the correct input and output settings, simply click the Capture button to create the capture.

You can click this button or use the hot keys. The default hot keys are CTRL+SHIFT+P. To view hotkey settings, choose Options → Program Preferences.

If you've chosen an Object or Window, SnagIt highlights the windows or objects on your screen with a red rectangle as you pass your cursor over them. When the correct object or window is highlighted, click the mouse and SnagIt captures that window or object.

Capturing Windows

Capturing entire windows is necessary to create the backdrop for your software demonstration. Every part of the demonstration should normally take place on top of a window capture of the software application.

To capture an entire window, follow these steps:

1　Choose the *Window* input option (Input → Window).

2　Choose the output option of your choice.

3　Click the Capture button or press the capture hotkeys (CTRL+SHIFT+P).

4　Move the mouse until you see a red rectangle appear around the window you want to capture.

5　Click the mouse button to create the capture.

That's it. You can now use that screen capture as part of the software demonstration.

Windows Tip: If you don't have a screen capture utility like SnagIt, you can capture windows to the clipboard by bringing the window to the forefront and pressing ALT+PRINTSCREEN.

Macintosh Tip: If you don't have a screen capture utility on you Mac, you can capture the screen, windows, or a defined rectangle to your hard drive by pressing COMMAND + SHIFT + 3 (entire screen), COMMAND + SHIFT + 4 (defined rectangle) or COMMAND + SHIFT + 4 + CAPSLOCK (window).

Capturing Objects

Capturing buttons or other elements such as toolbars is often helpful if you want to optimize the file size of each capture and of your demo. Instead of capturing the entire window, capturing just one button or one dropdown menu that changes can keep the files sizes much smaller.

To capture a button such as an OK button or another object, follow these steps:

1   Choose the *Object* input option (Input → Object).

2   Choose the output option of your choice.

3   Click the Capture button or press the capture hotkeys (CTRL+SHIFT+P).

4   Move the mouse until you see a red rectangle appear around the object you want to capture.

5   Click the mouse button to create the capture.

That's it. You have a small efficient capture of only the object that you need.

Capturing Menus

Capturing menus is necessary if you are demonstrating how to choose a certain option from a menu.

To capture a menu, such as the File menu in Dreamweaver, follow these steps:

1   Choose the *Menu* input option (Input → Menu).

2   Choose the output option of your choice.

3   Open the menu you are going to capture by clicking it.

4   Press the capture hotkeys (CTRL+SHIFT+P).

5   Place the cursor over the menu so it is highlighted.

6   Click the mouse button to create the capture.

There are two other settings that affect how menus are captured. To access these settings open the Input Properties dialog and select the Menu tab (Input → Properties → Menu):

Choose this setting to capture the menu bar just above the menu.

Choose this setting to capture menus that have multiple levels.

Input Properties   ✕

General | Fixed Region | Menu | Scrolling | TWAIN |

┌─ Menu Capture Options ─────────────────┐

☑ Include menu bar

☑ Capture cascaded menus

OK   Cancel   Apply   Help

Capturing a Region

Sometimes you need to capture a very specific part of the software application but it doesn't fall into the categories of window, object, or menu. For example, perhaps you need to capture just some selected text in a field. You can accomplish this by capturing a region that you define.

To capture a definable region, follow these steps:

1   Choose the *Region* input option (Input → Region).

2   Choose the output option of your choice.

3   Press the capture hotkeys (CTRL+SHIFT+P).

SnagIt changes the cursor to a crosshairs and displays a small window at the top left of the screen. In this small window you can see an enlarged image of the area around your cursor.

The purpose of this enlarged image is so that you can accurately capture all parts of an element on the screen.

4 Click and drag the cursor to create a rectangle around the area you want to capture.

When you release the mouse button SnagIt makes the capture.

Capturing the Mouse

When demonstrating software, the image that most often guides the learner through the demonstration is the mouse. In exercises later in this book, you will place the mouse on a timeline and animate it. You will then synchronize other events with the mouse. To do this you need to have a graphic of the mouse.

To create a screen capture of the mouse, follow these steps:

1 Place your mouse on a solid background.

For example, open a blank word document and use the white document as the background.

2 Choose the *Region* input option (Input → Region).

3 Set the Output option to *Clipboard*.

4 Choose to include the cursor in the SnagIt screen capture by choosing Include Cursor from the Input menu (Input → Include Cursor).

5 Press the **Capture** button or press the capture hotkeys (CTRL+SHIFT+P).

6   Use SnagIt to capture the region just around the mouse.

7   Paste the image into your favorite image-editing program.

8   Create a GIF image and make the background behind the mouse image transparent.

Making the background transparent ensures that as the mouse image travels over screen captures of other parts of the software, it won't obscure them.

 On CD: You are welcome to use the mouse GIF image that we've provided for use with the exercises. You can find it in on the CD as *mouse.gif*.

Using the File Output Option to Speed Up the Capture Process

One extremely nice feature that SnagIt offers is the ability to automatically create sequentially numbered files out of the screen captures it takes. This can save you loads of time by allowing you to skip the steps of opening a graphics editing program, pasting in the screen capture, and saving the file to the correct directory.

When you choose the *File* output setting, you are also telling SnagIt to use some related settings. To view these settings open the Output Settings dialog (Output → Properties → Image File):

Choose the type of image file you want SnagIt to create out of the capture.

For the quickest captures, have SnagIt name the files automatically for you.

Choose the folder where the captures should be automatically saved.

Output Properties ✕

Printer | Image File | Send Mail | Catalog Browser | Web

File Format
- BMP - Windows Bitmap
- GIF - CompuServe GIF
- JPG - JPEG Image
- PCX - PC Paintbrush
- PNG - Portable Network Graphics
- TGA - Truevision Targa
- TIF - Tagged Image File

Options...

File Name
- ○ Ask for File Name
- ○ Fixed File Name
  - Name: SNAGIT .GIF
- ● Automatic File Name
  - Prefix: SNAG- #.GIF
  - Number of digits in index: 1

Output Folder:
C:\test\DW sw Demo\

OK | Cancel | Apply | Help

Note: You might consider choosing the Ask for File Name option so you can name the file with an intelligible name for later reference. For sheer speed, use the prefix. SnagIt will name the file for you.

When you use the File output option, you can choose to have SnagIt automatically name your files for you. All of the files in this example that begin with the *SNAG* prefix were created using this option:

Name	Size	Type	Modified
mouse.gif	1 KB	GIF Image	6/17/2002 7:22 AM
mouseblip.gif	3 KB	GIF Image	9/14/2002 2:40 PM
SNAG-1.gif	2 KB	GIF Image	9/5/2002 11:19 AM
SNAG-2.gif	2 KB	GIF Image	9/5/2002 11:20 AM
SNAG-3.gif	6 KB	GIF Image	9/5/2002 11:21 AM
SNAG-4.gif	6 KB	GIF Image	9/5/2002 11:21 AM
SNAG-5.gif	6 KB	GIF Image	9/5/2002 11:21 AM
SNAG-6.gif	6 KB	GIF Image	9/5/2002 11:21 AM
SNAG-7.gif	13 KB	GIF Image	9/14/2002 2:57 PM
SNAG-8.gif	18 KB	GIF Image	9/14/2002 2:47 PM
sw_demo_sample...	10 KB	Microsoft HTML Doc...	9/14/2002 8:49 PM

Once you have created a sequential list of screen captures, they will be easy to import into Dreamweaver for the demonstration.

Note: All screen captures needed to complete exercises in this book have already been created for you

Screen Capture File Structure

If you are creating multiple software demonstrations for a single online course, it may be helpful to organize your screen capture image files.

Note: Remember that unlike other e-learning development tools that require you to import images into a proprietary environment, such as Flash, Dreamweaver creates HTML pages that references the screen capture images wherever they are placed within the site.

Our recommendation is to place all of your screen captures within a subfolder of the *images* directory called *screencaps*. Beneath that directory, create a separate subfolder for each demonstration and name the subfolders accordingly.

For example, if you have three demonstrations for using Microsoft Word that teach how to create a new file, how to open an existing file, and how to save a file, your screen capture file system might look something like this:

- images/screencaps/newfile/…
- images/screencaps/openfile/…
- images/screencaps/savefile/…

Summary

Creating screen captures is the first step in creating an HTML-based software demonstration. Though you don't have to use SnagIt as a screen capture utility, its ability to identify and capture certain Windows objects and menus, as well as its automatic image file creation and naming capabilities make it an excellent tool for this purpose.

Placing the Screen Captures on the Page 2

Once you've finished creating the screen captures and have placed them in a common directory, you need to place the screen captures in HTML layers so you can show and hide them at the appropriate times.

In this chapter you learn how to:

- Create, name, and position HTML layers.
- Place images in layers.
- Modify the layer stacking order (called the Z-index)

Layer Basics

HTML was originally a static environment in which text and images were placed on the page using tables. This is still the most common way to layout an HTML page. Layers were created to give web designers the ability to place page elements in exact fixed locations. The x and y coordinate properties allow exact positioning. The layer's position can also be changed on the fly, creating the potential for movement.

You can use Dreamweaver behaviors to dynamically change or hide and show layers. This makes it possible to create very interesting interactions and demonstrations.

You can also stack layers on top of each other, creating a three-dimensional work space. This stacking order property is called the *Z-index*.

Finally, Dreamweaver's timeline tools allow the layers to be moved based on time, creating the potential for showing a sequentially ordered demonstration.

Creating Layers

To create a layer using Dreamweaver, select the Layer tool then click and drag the mouse to draw a layer.

To create a layer, follow these steps:

1   In Dreamweaver, select the Layer tool.

You can find this tool on the Common tab.

Dreamweaver changes the cursor to cross hairs.

2   Click and drag the mouse to create the size of layer you need.

2   Release the mouse.

Dreamweaver creates the layer and places the cursor inside it:

Naming Layers

To demonstrate certain software tasks, you might end up creating dozens of layers. Make sure to name the layers so that when you work with them later on you will know which layer to use.

To name a layer, follow these steps:

1   Open the Layers panel (Window → Others → Layers).

Make sure the Layers tab is selected so the Layers panel is showing.

If there is a closed-eye image next to the layer it is hidden. If not, it is visible.

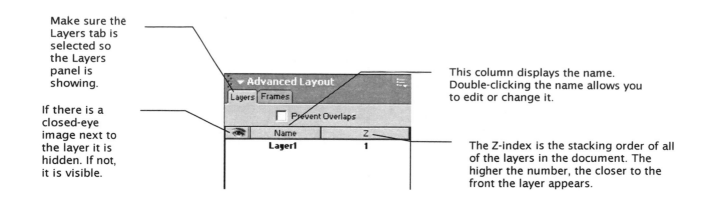

This column displays the name. Double-clicking the name allows you to edit or change it.

The Z-index is the stacking order of all of the layers in the document. The higher the number, the closer to the front the layer appears.

2   Double-click the name of the layer you want to edit.

Dreamweaver highlights the default name in the Name field:

3   Enter the new name for the layer and press ENTER.

Dreamweaver displays the new name in the Layers panel:

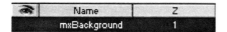

Positioning Layers

Positioning layers is crucial to a smooth demonstration. You want the learner to have the illusion that the actual software application is being used, so you need to make sure all successive screen shots line up perfectly with each other. If not the learner will notice a shift as you hide and show the layers.

Follow these steps to position a layer:

1   Select the layer by clicking its border or tab.

When a layer is selected, you will see select boxes all around the layer as shown here:

Click either the border or the tab to select the layer.

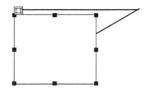

If the layer contains an image, and you click in the middle of the layer, you will only select the image, and it will display as shown here:

   ——————— The layer tab.

Notice that select boxes do not surround the layer. If you have selected the image, just click the layer tab to reselect the layer.

2   Move the layer to its correct position. You can do this by clicking the layer tab and dragging with the mouse or by selecting the layer and using the arrow keys to move it in small increments.

 Tip: You can also position a layer by changing the Left and Top properties using the Properties inspector. This can be very helpful when you need to move a layer to an exact position.

▼ Properties							
Layer ID	L 30px	V 256px	Z-Index 1	Bg Image			
MainStage	T 110px	H 198px	Vis visible	Bg Color			
Tag DIV	Overflow	Clip L	R				
		T	B				

Inserting Screen Captures Into Layers

Once you've created a layer, you need to insert the appropriate screen capture into the layer.

To insert an image into a layer, follow these steps:

1   Click inside the layer to place the cursor inside the layer.

2   Click the Image icon in the Common category of the Insert panel or choose Insert → Image.

3   Browse for and select the image you want. Click **OK** (**Open** on a Mac) to insert the image.

Dreamweaver places the image inside the layer with the image selected:

 Note: Dreamweaver expands the layer size to accommodate the size of the image.

Changing the Stacking Order (Z-Index) of Layers

Each layer in a document has an associated property called the Z-index. This property controls the layer's stacking order relative to other layers. If the Z-index is a high number, the layer will appear closer to the top or front of the stack. Lower numbers appear closer to the bottom or back of the stack.

The Z-index property gives layers a three dimensional property. This is especially important when you consider that the mouse image needs to always appear in front of all the other screen captures.

To change the stacking order of layers, follow these steps:

1   Open the Layers panel (Windows → Others → Layers).

2   Click the layer's Z-index field.

Dreamweaver places the cursor in the field and selects the current value:

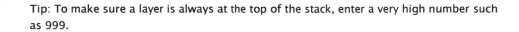

3   Enter the new value and press ENTER.

 Tip: To make sure a layer is always at the top of the stack, enter a very high number such as 999.

Hands–On: Setting Up the Layers for the Demonstration

As you work through the exercises in this book, you will create a functioning software demonstration. Each chapter contains exercises that will contribute to the final software demonstration. The focus of this demonstration is to show how to save a document as a different name using the Save As option in the File menu of Dreamweaver MX.

The layers and screenshots have already been created for you. In this exercise you will position the layers and make sure the stacking order is correct.

Viewing the Finished Exercise

Before completing the steps for this exercise, take a look at how the finished page should look when you are done.

 On CD: Open and explore /sample_2/sample_2-1.htm.

When looking at this file, look closely at where the layers are positioned, what their z-index properties are, and what their visibility property is.

Setting Up the Layers

This hands-on exercise will have three main steps that must be completed for each layer:

- Positioning the layer.
- Setting the z-index property for the layer.
- Setting the visibility property for the layer.

Follow these-steps to set up the screen shot layers:

1 Create a new Dreamweaver site and point the local directory to the files accompanying this book.

More Information: You can find detailed instructions on how to set up a new site in our book titled Fundamental e-Learning Techniques Using Dreamweaver. You can find more details about this book at the Rapid Intake Press website (*www.rapidintakepress.com*).

2 Open /sample_2/sample_2-1_Start.htm.

This file already contains all of the layers and screenshots necessary to successfully create the software demo:

The layers panel displays all of the existing layers.

Remember to click and drag the layer handle when re-positioning a layer.

3 To begin positioning the layers, set the visibility property of all layers to *hidden* except for the layer titled MainStage.

👁	Name	Z
🖉	mouse	999
🖉	FinalImage	10
🖉	SaveAsSav...	9
🖉	saveAsBlan...	8
🖉	saveAs	7
🖉	MainStage2	6
🖉	menu7	4
🖉	menu6	3
🖉	menu5	3
🖉	menu4	3
🖉	menu3	3
🖉	menu2	3
🖉	menu1	3
🖉	fileButton	2
👁	MainStage	1

Tip: A quick way to accomplish this is to click the eye icon at the top of the visibility property column in the Layers panel. Dreamweaver automatically sets the visibility property of all layers to hidden. Then click the MainStage layer eye icon until it appear opened indicating the visible value.

4 Set the position in pixels of the MainStage layer to *Left = 30* and *Top = 110*.

Left and Top refer
to the number of
pixels from the top
left-hand corner of
the screen.

This sets the position of the main screenshot that most of the other screenshots will appear on top of.

The mouse will move to the File menu, so we need to place the File menu raised button to mimic the appearance of the button changing states when the mouse passes over it.

5 Set the visibility property of the fileButton layer to *visible*.

6 Set the position in pixels of the fileButton layer to *Left = 54* and *Top = 133*.

How did we come up with the numbers 54,133? We simply moved the layer by hand to the correct position on the screen and checked the property panel.

Now we need to display and position the File menu screen captures.

7 Set the visibility property of the Menu1 layer to *visible*, and the position properties to *Left = 54* and *Top = 154*.

8   Show the menu2 layer. Set its position to *58, 157 (Left = 58* and *Top = 157).*

We use the menu images to highlight the menu options as the cursor passes over them.

Tip: **Notice that screen captures to highlight the menu options consist only of the menu option itself and not the entire menu. This helps keep the file size of the demonstration to a minimum.**

9   Show the menu3 layer. Set its position to *57,172.*

10   Show the menu4 layer. Set its position to *57,191.*

11   Show the menu5 layer. Set its position to *55, 207.*

12   Show the menu6 layer. Set its position to *56, 233.*

13   Show the menu7 layer. Set its position to *57, 251.*

Once the mouse passes over the Save As option, we're going to display the Save As dialog. This is because at that point in the demonstration we will have the mouse select that menu option.

14 Show layer saveAs. Set its position to *160, 170*.

15 Show layer saveAsBlankField. Set its position to *243, 506*.

This is the blank field we will use to enter the name of the file.

16 Show layer SaveAsSaveButton. Set its position to *687,506*.

The image in this layer will allow us to animate the **Save** button.

Now we're ready to position the final image.

17 Show layer FinalImage. Set its position to *30, 110*.

 Note: You may be wondering, "How did they come up with all of these exact numbers for the positioning?" We simply moved the layers into an approximate position, then adjusted the position using the arrow keys until the layers all appear in the correct position.

The last layer we need to position is the layer containing the mouse. We need to place the mouse where it should be at the beginning of the demo. Let's start it off at the bottom right-hand side of the application screen capture. Starting the mouse a long ways from its first target allows the learner to view the mouse in motion before other actions occur.

18 Show the mouse layer. Set its position to *630, 680*.

Good, you've displayed all of the layers and positioned them correctly. Now you need to make sure the stacking order is correct. We've done a lot of this for you, but just to be sure, make sure the z-index matches what we show here:

	mouse	999
	FinalImage	10
	SaveAsSaveButton	9
	saveAsBlankField	8
	saveAs	7
	menu7	4
	menu6	3
	menu5	3
	menu4	3
	menu3	3
	menu2	3
	menu1	3
	fileButton	2
	MainStage	1

19 Adjust the stacking order if necessary by setting the z-index property of each layer.

The last thing you need to do is get the layers ready for the demonstration by hiding all but the background layer (mainStage) and the mouse layer.

20 Hide all of the layers except the MainStage and mouse layers.

👁	Name	Z
👁	mouse	999
⊜	FinalImage	10
⊜	SaveAsSaveButton	9
⊜	saveAsBlankField	8
⊜	saveAs	7
⊜	menu7	4
⊜	menu6	3
⊜	menu5	3
⊜	menu4	3
⊜	menu3	3
⊜	menu2	3
⊜	menu1	3
⊜	fileButton	2
👁	MainStage	1

Summary

In this chapter you learned how to work with layers. Layers allow us to hide and show screen captures as well as animate the mouse image. (You'll learn how to animate the mouse in a later chapter).

With the layers stacked and positioned correctly we are ready to move onto the next step, which is using the Dreamweaver timeline to assemble the demonstration.

Using Dreamweaver Timelines to Assemble the Demonstration

3

After you have stacked and positioned the layers that contain the screen captures, you are ready to start working with the timeline. Using Dreamweaver timelines allows you to animate the mouse as well as indicate when you want certain layers to show and hide.

In this chapter you learn how to:

- Add the mouse layer to a timeline.
- Move the mouse layer using a timeline.
- Trigger behavior actions at specific points on a timeline to show and hide the screen captures.
- Use JavaScript to mimic the typing text.

Hands-on: Animating the Mouse

To animate the mouse layer (make it move across the page), you need to place it on a timeline. A Dreamweaver timeline is a tool you can use to animate any layer in a web page based on the number of seconds since the timeline started playing. Timelines allow you to synchronize multiple events happening on a web page (such as the mouse layer moving and other screen capture layers showing and hiding). Dreamweaver supplies several built-in behaviors you can use to control timelines.

Viewing the Finished Exercise

Before completing the steps for this exercise, take a look at how the page should look when you are done with this exercise.

On CD: Open and explore /sample_2/sample_2-2.htm.

When viewing this sample, open and explore the timeline panel (Window → Others → Timeline).

Add and Animate the Mouse Layer on a Timeline

To add the mouse layer to a timeline, follow these steps:

1   Using Dreamweaver, open /sample_2/sample_2-2_start.htm.

Note: This file begins where the exercise in chapter 2 left off. If you successfully completed the exercise in chapter 2, you may want to use your own file instead.

2   Select the mouse layer.

3   Add the layer to a timeline (Modify → Timeline → Add Object to Timeline).

Dreamweaver displays this tip indicating which layer properties you can change in a timeline.

Dreamweaver also adds the object to the timeline and displays the timeline panel:

Playback head

The name of the timeline.

Use these playback controls to step through the timeline frame by frame.

FPS is the number of Frames Per Second. Higher numbers slow down the timeline, lower numbers speed it up.

The *Behaviors* Channel. Add behaviors to this line to indicate when to show and hide screen captures.

Choose *Loop* if you want the timeline to start over when it reaches the last frame.

This name refers to the name of the layer placed on the timeline

Animation Channels. Each animated layer is placed on a different channel.

These circles indicate *keyframes*. Keyframes indicate beginning and ending animation points.

Choose *Autoplay* to start the timeline as soon as the page loads in the browser.

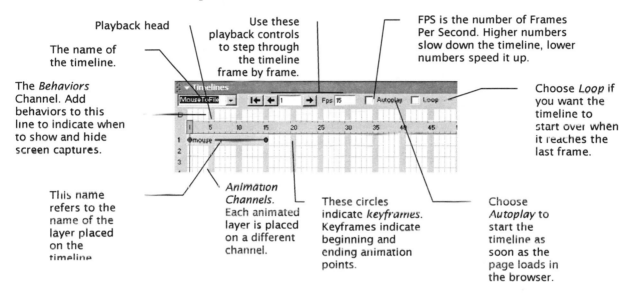

 Note: Notice that the layer is added to the timeline using a default duration of one second (15 frames in this case).

4   Select the last keyframe in the first animation channel by clicking it.

Dreamweaver moves the playback head to frame 15:

5 In the document window, click and drag the mouse layer until its pointer is directly over the file menu of the background screen capture.

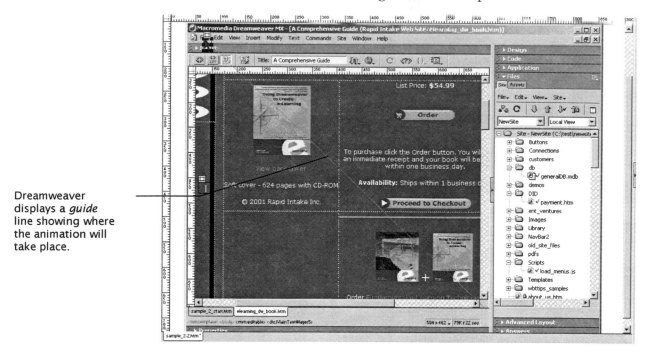

Dreamweaver displays a *guide* line showing where the animation will take place.

Tip: You can test your animation by clicking the playback controls.

Hands-on: Adding Behaviors to the Timeline to Show and Hide Screen Captures

Once you've animated the mouse, you have a reference point from which you can show and hide the other screen captures. You do this based upon the mouse's position.

Viewing the Finished Exercise

Before completing the steps for this exercise, take a look at how the page should look when you are done.

On CD: Open and explore /*sample_2/sample_2-3.htm*.

When viewing this sample, open and explore the timeline panel (Window → Others → Timeline).

Add Behavior Actions to the Timeline

Now you'll use behaviors to hide and show the screen captures that correspond with the mouse's movement.

Note: When adding behaviors to a timeline, it is important that you remember to select frames in the behavior channel, not in the animation channel.

1 To add a show/hide behavior to a timeline, follow these steps:Using Dreamweaver, open /sample_2/sample_2-3_start.htm.

Note: This file begins where the last exercise left off. If you successfully completed the last exercise, you may want to use your own file instead.

2 Open the timeline panel and select frame 15 in the behaviors channel.

The black highlight indicates that the frame is selected.

Frame 15 is the point on the timeline that the mouse image passes over the File menu, so we need to display the FileButton layer to simulate the mouseover effect of a Windows menubar.

3 Open the Behaviors panel and add a Show-Hide Layers behavior.

Dreamweaver displays the Show-Hide Layers dialog:

4   Select layer fileButton and click **Show** and click **OK**.

Dreamweaver displays the behavior event and action in the Behaviors panel:

The event indicates that when the timelines gets to frame 15, this Show-Hide Layers action will occur.

Tip: You may find it helpful to test your demonstration at several different points during your development. An easy way to test it is to select the Autoplay setting on the Timeline panel, and then preview the Dreamweaver page in a browser (F12).

Now that we have the mouse moving to the file menu and the file menu button "popping up," we are ready to show the file menu.

5   In the Timeline panel, select frame 20 in the behavior channel.

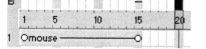

We use frame 20 instead of frame 15 to allow for time associated with a mouse click before something else happens. In a later exercise we will highlight the mouse click more clearly.

6   Add a Show-Hide Layers behavior and show the *menu1* layer.

Your behavior channel should look like this:

Now we need to continue to animate the mouse layer to show the mouse moving down the File menu.

7   Click on the playback head and move it to frame 25. Then select the *mouse* layer in the Layers panel.

8   Add the mouse layer to the timeline (Modify → Timeline → Add Object to Timeline).

Dreamweaver adds the object to the same animation channel:

9   Set the visibility property of layer *menu1* to *visible*.

👁   menu1   3

Making layer *menu1* visible allows us to have a reference point so we know how far we need to move the mouse layer to get to the Save As option.

10 Select the last keyframe on frame 39.

11 Click and drag the mouse layer until it is over the Save As option in the File menu.

With the mouse animation set, we are ready to add more Show-Hide Layer behaviors to the timeline to show the menu option highlighting as the mouse passes over them.

12 On frame 26 add a Show-Hide Layers behavior. Show layer *menu2* and hide layer *fileButton*.

13 On frame 29 add a behavior to show layer *menu3* and hide layer *menu2*.

14 On frame 31 add a behavior to show layer *menu4* and hide layer *menu3*.

15 On frame 33 add a behavior to show layer *menu5* and hide layer *menu4*.

16 On frame 36 add a behavior to show layer *menu6* and hide layer *menu5*.

17 On frame 38 add a behavior to show layer *menu7* and hide layer *menu6*.

Tip: If you accidentally place the behavior in the wrong frame, you can drag it to the correct frame.

Now we're ready to test the demonstration up to this point.

18 On the timeline, select *Autoplay*. Then, using the Layers panel, hide layer *menu1* and preview the page in a browser (F12).

You should see the demonstration start automatically. The mouse should move to the File menu, the File menu should appear, and as the mouse moves down the file menu you should see each option highlighted. If you want to view the demonstration again, refresh your browser window.

Hands-on: Using JavaScript to Mimic Typing Text

In many software demonstration you need to not only show mouse movement, but text entry as well. You can, of course, simply show a screenshot with the text already there, but to create the appearance of actually working in the real software application you need to mimic the text being typed into the field.

You don't need to know JavaScript to make this happen. Simply follow the steps in this section and you'll be able to add typing text to the demo in no time!

Viewing the Finished Exercise

Before completing the steps for this exercise, take a look at how the page should look when you are done.

On CD: Open and explore /sample_2/sample_2-4.htm.

When viewing this sample, watch what happens in the File Name field of the Save As dialog—the demonstration simulates the effect of typing text.

Using JavaScript to Simulate Typing Text

The last exercise left the mouse over the Save As option in the File menu. We now need to hide the menu, display the Save As dialog, show the new filename being typed into the File Name field, and have the mouse move to the **Save** button. Once the mouse moves over the save button, we can close the Save As dialog and display the final screen capture that displays the changed filename.

To use JavaScript to simulate typing text, follow these steps:

1 Using Dreamweaver, open /sample_2/sample_2-4_start.htm.

Note: This file begins where the last exercise left off. If you successfully completed the last exercise, you may want to use your own file instead.

2   Open the timeline panel and on frame 44 use a behavior to hide layer *menu7* and *menu1*, and show layer *saveAs*.

3   On frame 60, use a behavior to show layer *saveAsBlankField*.

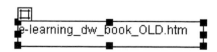

We are showing the *saveAsBlankField* layer so that when we make the text appear as if it is being typed in the field, it won't be displayed over the existing text in the File Name field.

Showing this field accomplishes two things. First, it clears the previous text that was showing in the File name field. This would normally happen once a user starts typing text or presses delete. Second, it provides a blank background for displaying the typed text.

4   Using the Layers panel, show the *saveAs* and *saveAsBlankField* layers in Dreamweaver design view.

Showing these layers gives us a guide for positioning the typing text.

5   Using the layer tool, create a new layer somewhere on the page and enter this text into it: *elearning_dw_book_OLD.htm*.

e-learning_dw_book_OLD.htm

More Information: See Chapter 2: Placing the Screen Captures on the Page for more information about how to create and work with layers.

6   Using the Layers panel, name the layer *typingText* and set its z-index value to *11*.

👁	Name	Z
👁	mouse	999
	typingText	11
📄	FinalImage	10
📄	SaveAsSaveButton	9
📄	saveAsBlankField	9

7   Attach the style sheet **styles.css** to the current page (Text → CSS Styles → Attach Style Sheet).

Dreamweaver displays the style *typingText* in the CSS panel:

 More Information: You can find more details about CSS styles and how you can apply them to e-learning course development in our other titles Fundamental e-Learning Techniques Using Dreamweaver MX and Using Dreamweaver to Create e-Learning: A Comprehensive Guide to CourseBuilder and Learning Site. See the Rapid Intake Press website for more information (www.rapidintakepress.com).

8   With the *typingText* layer still selected, open the CSS panel, and click the *typingText* style to apply it to the layer.

Applying this style ensures that the text we are going to "type" into the File Name field appears more like the rest of the text in the Save As dialog.

9   Drag the *typingText* layer over the *SaveAsBlankField* layer and position it so that the text appears to be inside the File Name field.

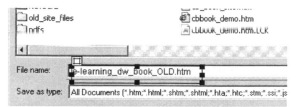

10 Delete the text from inside the *typingText* layer. This text will be added on the fly using JavaScript.

11 Click Dreamweaver's **Show Code View** button.

Dreamweaver displays the page's code.

12 Scroll to the top of the document and paste the following code just after the first script tag.

On CD: You can find this code on the CD in the typing_text.js file.

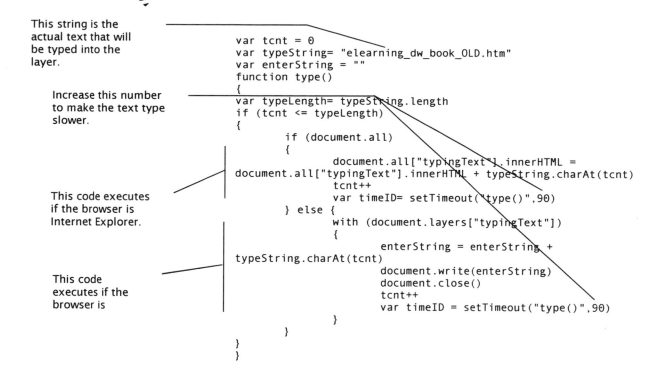

This string is the actual text that will be typed into the layer.

Increase this number to make the text type slower.

This code executes if the browser is Internet Explorer.

This code executes if the browser is

```
var tcnt = 0
var typeString= "elearning_dw_book_OLD.htm"
var enterString = ""
function type()
{
var typeLength= typeString.length
if (tcnt <= typeLength)
{
        if (document.all)
        {
                document.all["typingText"].innerHTML =
document.all["typingText"].innerHTML + typeString.charAt(tcnt)
                tcnt++
                var timeID= setTimeout("type()",90)
        } else {
                with (document.layers["typingText"])
                {
                        enterString = enterString +
typeString.charAt(tcnt)
                        document.write(enterString)
                        document.close()
                        tcnt++
                        var timeID = setTimeout("type()",90)
                }
        }
}
}
```

This screen shot shows you where in the document you need to past the code:

Paste the text here.

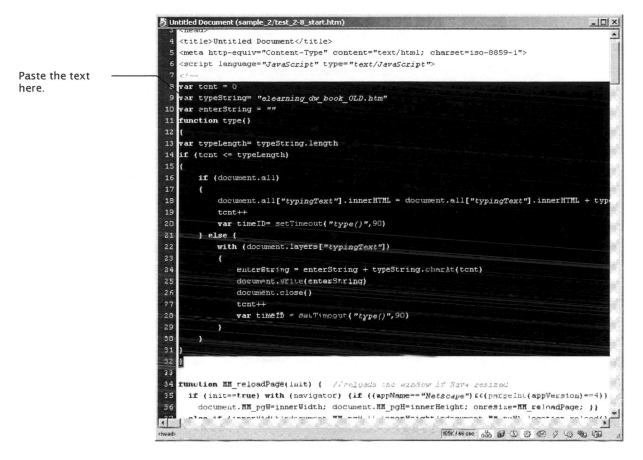

```
Untitled Document (sample_2/test_2-8_start.htm)                          _ □ ×
 3  <head>
 4  <title>Untitled Document</title>
 5  <meta http-equiv="Content-Type" content="text/html; charset=iso-8859-1">
 6  <script language="JavaScript" type="text/JavaScript">
 7  <!--
 8  var tcnt = 0
 9  var typeString= "elearning_dw_book_OLD.htm"
10  var enterString = ""
11  function type()
12  {
13  var typeLength= typeString.length
14  if (tcnt <= typeLength)
15  {
16      if (document.all)
17      {
18          document.all["typingText"].innerHTML = document.all["typingText"].innerHTML + typ
19          tcnt++
20          var timeID= setTimeout("type()",90)
21      } else {
22          with (document.layers["typingText"])
23          {
24              enterString = enterString + typeString.charAt(tcnt)
25              document.write(enterString)
26              document.close()
27              tcnt++
28              var timeID = setTimeout("type()",90)
29          }
30      }
31  }
32  }
33
34  function MM_reloadPage(init) {  //reloads the window if Nav4 resized
35    if (init==true) with (navigator) {if ((appName=="Netscape")&&(parseInt(appVersion)==4))
36      document.MM_pgW=innerWidth; document.MM_pgH=innerHeight; onresize=MM_reloadPage; }}
```
<head>   165K / 46 sec

 Note: Whenever you use this code as is, just make sure the layer you want the text to type into is called "typingText". This script was modified from a script found at www.htmlgoodies.com.

Describing this code in detail is beyond the purpose of this book. However, a general description may be helpful for those that are familiar with JavaScript.

When this function is called it first checks to see if the counter is greater than the number of characters that must be typed. Then it does a check to find out which browser is being used.

The code differs depending upon whether the browser is Internet Explorer or Netscape Navigator. In Internet Explorer, one character is added to the innerHTML property of the layer each time the function is called. In Netscape, a variable is written to the layer each time the function is called. The variable is updated with a new character each time the function is called.

The setTimeout function, calls the type() function again after a certain amount of time. The time entered represents milliseconds. This process continues until the counter is greater than the number of characters in the text.

Now lets continue with the exercise.

13 On frame 65 of the timeline panel, add a behavior to show the *typingText* layer.

14 On frame 65, also add a Call JavaScript behavior. When Dreamweaver prompts you for the code, enter *type()*. This will call the type function for the first time.

You should now have two behaviors that will happen when the timeline reaches frame 65:

15 Move the timeline playhead to frame 85.

16 Select the *mouse* layer and add it to the timeline (Modify → Timeline → Add Object to Timeline).

17 Select the last keyframe on frame 99.

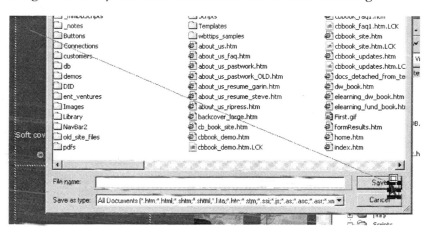

18 Drag the *mouse* layer over the Save button on the Save As dialog.

19 On frame 110, add a behavior that shows the layer *SaveAsSaveButton*.

This mimics the clicking of the button.

20 On frame 114, add a behavior that shows the *finalImage* layer, hides the *saveAs* layer, hides the *saveAsBlankField* layer, hides the *SaveAsSaveButton* layer, and hides the *typingText* layer.

21 Test your document by previewing it in a browser.

That's It! You've completed a basic demo using Dreamweaver!

Summary

In this chapter you added the mouse layer to the timeline so you could animate it. You learned how to add behaviors to the timeline and you learned how to use JavaScript to simulate the typing of text.

To get this far you had to complete dozens of detailed steps. But remember that there are really only a few general steps. Let's review the general steps you've followed so far:

1 Take screen captures of all steps in the demonstration.

2   Place each of these screen captures in a layer and stack them according to the order they will appear in the demonstration.

3   Create a mouse image, place it in a layer, and set its Z-index to *999* so that it always appears on top of the other images.

4   Add the mouse image to a Dreamweaver timeline.

5   Animate the mouse using the timeline and at the appropriate positions, add **Show/Hide Layers** behaviors to the timeline to show the layers that contain the screenshots.

6   Either start the timeline automatically by choosing the *Autoplay* option on the timeline panel, or start the timeline based on another event by using the **Start Timeline** behavior. You've only used the Autoplay option thus far. In a later chapter you'll learn how to use behaviors to control the timeline.

Enhancing the Demonstration 4

Now that you've completed your first demonstration, let's take a look at a couple of ways to enhance the demo.

In this chapter you learn how to:

- Use animated GIFs to illustrate the mouse clicks.
- Add annotations to explain or point out concepts as the demonstration progresses.
- Add mouse-click sounds and synchronized audio to the demonstration.

Hands–On: Illustrating Mouse Clicks

If you've completed all of the exercises in this book, your demonstration works fairly well. However, there is no indication when mouse clicks occur in the demonstration.

For example, when the mouse passes over the file menu the demonstration should make it apparent that a mouse click occurs to make the file menu appear. This could be an unnecessary step in this particular case, given that most users are going to know a mouse click is required to display a menu. On the other hand, illustrating the mouse clicks will make the demonstration easier to understand. And even if you don't want to use them when demonstrating a menu structure, you may need to use them for other software tasks that are not as intuitive.

In this exercise you will show and hide animated GIFs at certain points along the timeline to demonstrate when the mouse is clicked.

Viewing the Finished Exercise

Before completing the steps for this exercise, take a look at how the page should look when you are done.

On CD: Open and explore /sample_2/sample_2-5.htm.

When viewing this sample, notice what happens when the mouse *clicks* the File menu, the Save As option, and the **Save** button on the Save As dialog.

Using Animated GIFs to Illustrate Mouse Clicks

There are many animations you could use to illustrate a mouse click. To animate this illustration we've chosen to use an animated GIF.

To use an animated GIF to illustrate mouse clicks, follow these steps:

1   Using Dreamweaver, open /sample_2/sample_2-5_start.htm.

Note: This file begins where the last exercise left off. If you successfully completed the last exercise, you may want to use your own file instead.

2   Create a new layer called *MouseHighlight* and set its z-index value to *12*.

3   Place the cursor inside the layer and insert the image *mouseblip.gif* into the layer (Insert → Image).

Dreamweaver displays the first frame of the animated GIF in the layer.

4   Move the layer so the circle displays directly over the File menu on the background screen capture.

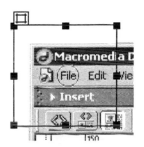

5   In frame 18 on the Timeline panel, add a behavior to show the *MouseHighlight* layer

6   Modify the behavior on frame 26 of the timeline to hide the *MouseHighlight* layer.

7   Use the Layers panel to hide the *MouseHighlight* layer and test your demonstration in a browser.

Note: The animated GIF will automatically start playing as soon as MouseHighlight layer is shown. If you didn't hide the MouseHighlight layer before testing it, the GIF may have finished its animation prematurely. In Netscape, the browser starts the animation as soon as the page loads, so you won't see this effect properly.

The demonstration should now show an animated circle growing larger when the mouse "clicks" the file menu.

Now we need to do the same thing for the mouse click on the Save As menu option and the **Save** button in the Save As dialog.

8 Create another layer with the *mouseblip.gif* image in it and name it *MouseHighlight2*. Set the Z-index to 12.

👁	mouse	999
👁	MouseHighlight2	12
	MouseHighlight	12
	typingText	11
	FinalImage	10

9 Using the Layers panel, show layer *menu1*.

This layer will server as a guide so we can know where to place the next animated GIF.

10 On the timeline, move the playback head to frame 39.

The mouse should be positioned over the Save As option in the File menu.

11 Drag the *MouseHighlight2* layer so that the center of the circle in the layer is directly over the top of the tip of the mouse.

12 On frame 39 of the timeline, add a behavior that shows layer *MouseHighlight2*.

13 On frame 47 of the timeline, add a behavior to hide layer *MouseHighlight2*.

14 Use the Layers panel to hide the *menu1* layer and the *MouseHighlight2* layer.

15 Create another layer with the *mouseblip.gif* image in it and name it
       MouseHighlight3. Set the Z-index to 12.

16 Using the Layers panel, show layer *saveAs*.

       This layer will server as a guide so we know where to place the next animated
       GIF.

17 On the timeline, move the playback head to frame 99.

       The mouse should be positioned over the Save button on the Save As dialog.

18 Drag the *MouseHighlight3* layer so that the center of the circle is directly over the
       top of the tip of the mouse.

19 Modify the behavior at frame 110 to show the *MouseHighlight3* layer.

20 Add a behavior at frame 118 to hide the *MouseHighlight3* layer.

21 Use the Layers panel to hide the *saveAs* and *MouseHighlight3* layers.

22 Test the demonstration in a browser.

You've successfully added animated GIFs to your demonstration to illustrate
mouse clicks.

Hands-on: Adding Annotations

Believe it or not, you already have the skills to add annotations to the
demonstration. To add an annotation, simply create a layer with an opaque
background, add some text. Then show and hide it at the appropriate times on the
timeline.

This may not be the nicest looking annotation, but it barely increases the file size of
the demonstration. If you would like to add a background graphic to the layer that
looks a little nicer, you may. You may also want to use this technique to add images
of arrows that point out features in the demonstration

In this exercise you will add an annotation that appears at the very end pointing out that the file name has changed in the Dreamweaver window.

Viewing the Finished Exercise

Before completing the steps for this exercise, take a look at how the page should look when you are done.

On CD: Open and explore /sample_2/sample_2-6.htm.

Using Layers to Add Annotations

To use layers to add annotations to the demonstration, follow these steps:

1   Using Dreamweaver, open /sample_2/sample_2-6_start.htm.

Note: This file begins where the last exercise left off. If you successfully completed the last exercise, you may want to use your own file instead.

2   Create a layer, name it *annotation*, and set its z-index value to *13*.

👁	Name	Z
👁	mouse	999
	annotation	13
	MouseHighlight3	12
	MouseHighlight2	12
	MouseHighlight	12

3   Click inside the layer and enter "When you are finished saving the document with a new name, Dreamweaver displays the new filename in the Windows title bar."

4   In the Properties inspector, choose a light-colored background for the layer.

Click here to choose the background color for the layer.

Properties

	Layer ID	L 327px	W 250px	Z-Index 13	Bg Image	
	annotation	T 133px	H 162px	Vis default	Bg Color	#FFFFCC
Tag DIV	Overflow		Clip L	R	
			T	B	

5   On frame 118 of the timeline, modify the Show-Hide layers behavior to show the *annotation* layer.

6   Using the layer panel, hide the *annotation* layer and test the demonstration in a browser.

Tip: To create a margin for the annotation, create two layers with identical backgrounds. Make one of them smaller. Place the smaller layer one on top of the larger layer. Show them both on the timeline at the same time. You've got a margin!

Tip: To make the annotation layer more visually appealing, create a drop shadow by either creating another layer with a black background and placing it directly behind the annotation layer or by applying a CSS style that uses Internet Explorer's filters. See /sample_2/sample_2-6_dropshadow.htm for a simple example of the first method.

Hands-On: Adding Sounds

You can further enhance your demonstration by adding Flash-based sounds. You can use sound to emphasize mouse clicks, add synchronized voice-over narration, or add other sound effects.

Note: Remember, when adding sound you almost always need to require the learner to have a plug-in. If your project requires a "plug-in free" course, you probably need to produce a "soundless" demo. We feel Flash offers the very best way to add sound to e-learning pages because of the pervasive browser penetration by the Flash Player plug-in.

If you are a Flash developer, you may want to know how we created the audio files. We first inserted a streaming audio object on a new layer. We put a stop action on the first frame so it doesn't play the audio right away. We also put a stop action on the last frame to make sure the audio didn't loop.

Viewing the Finished Exercise

Before completing the steps for this exercise, take a look at how the page should look when you are done.

On CD: Open and explore /sample_2/sample_2-7.htm.

Adding Sound to the Demonstration

In this exercise you will add a mouse-click sound and a voice over to the demonstration.

To add sound to the demonstration, follow these steps:

1   Using Dreamweaver, open /sample_2/sample_2-7_start.htm.

Note: This file begins where the last exercise left off. If you successfully completed the last exercise, you may want to use your own file instead.

2   Place your cursor just after the instruction text at the top of the page and insert the Flash file *mouseclick.swf*.

Add the flash file by clicking and dragging the file from the file list, by using the menus (Insert → Media → Flash), or by clicking the Flash icon on the Insert panel.

Dreamweaver displays an icon representing the Flash file's position on the page:

3   In the Properties panel, name the object *mouseclick*.

Enter the name of the object here.

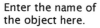

We have found that the
Autoplay property does
not always effectively
control whether or not
the movie begins
playing immediately or
not. So we decided to
control that behavior
with actions in the Flash
movie itself.

Properties

	Flash, 1K	W 5	File ../mouseclick.swf		Edit...
	mouseclick	H 5	Src /mouseclick.fla		Reset Size
☑ Loop	V Space	Quality High	Align Default	▷ Play
☑ Autoplay	H Space	Scale Default (Show all)	Bg	Parameters...

Note: You must name the object to be able to control it using the Control Shockwave or
Flash behavior.

4   Insert the Flash file voiceover.swf immediately after the mouseclick object.

Dreamweaver shows icons for both Flash files:

⊔⊔⊔⊔⊔⊔⊔⊔⊔⊔⊔⊔⊔⊔⊔⊔⊔⊔⊔

⟩ change the name ⟨

.o:

Note: The only thing these Flash files contain is the sound file. The background is white so
they do not appear visible on the web page.

5   Name the new Flash object *voice*.

Properties

	Flash, 8K	W
	voice	H
☑ Loop	V Space

6   On the timeline, add a Control Shockwave or Flash behavior to frame 18.

7   Choose *movie "mouseclick"* from the dropdown list and *Play* as the action and
click **OK**.

Control Shockwave or Flash   ✕

Movie: [movie "mouseclick" ▼]   [OK]

Action: ⦿ Play   ○ Stop   [Cancel]
        ○ Rewind   ○ Go to Frame [   ]   [Help]

Adding this behavior at this frame causes the audio to play at the same time we are highlighting the mouse click.

For frame 18 you should see two behaviors in the Behaviors panel:

Events	Actions
onFrame18	Show-Hide Layers
onFrame18	Control Shockwave or F

8   Add the same Control Shockwave or Flash behavior to frames 39 and 110—the other two times the mouse demonstrates a click in the demo.

Now we are ready to add the voice over audio.

9   Add a Control Shockwave or Flash behavior to frame 5 to start the voice over narration. Choose *movie "voice"* from the dropdown list and *Play* as the action and click **OK**.

10 Test the demo in a browser. You should hear the voice over and mouse click audio files play at the appropriate times.

Summary

To help illustrate when the mouse is clicked in a demonstration, you may want to use some kind of visual clue. In this chapter you learned how to add an animated GIF to illustrate the clicking of the mouse.

In addition, annotations can help make a software demonstration more effective. You also learned how to add annotations to a demonstration using the show/hide layer behavior in the timeline, and you learned a few tips for making the annotations more appealing.

Finally, sound can be used to illustrate mouse clicks or play a voice-over narration. You learned how to add Flash-based audio files to the document and control when they are played using the Control Shockwave or Flash behavior.

Adding Learner Controls 5

You may want to give the learner some ability to control the demonstration. You can do this with buttons that let the learner start, stop and replay the demonstration.

In this chapter you learn how to:

- Use the Autoplay feature to start the demo when the page loads.
- Create clickable images that allow the learner to start, stop, and replay the demonstration.

Using Autoplay to Automatically Start the Demo

Select this option to start the demo when the page loads.

If you want to start the demonstration when the page loads, use the Autoplay option. You can find the Autoplay option on the Timeline panel:

▼ Timelines							
MouseToFile ▼	|◄	◄ |1	→	Fps |15	☑ Autoplay	☐ Loop

B

| 1 | 5 | 10 | 15 | 20 | 25 | 30 | 35 | 40 | 45 | 50 |

1   Omouse ————————O   Omouse ————————O

2

This is the option we have been using up to this point.

Hands On: Using Buttons to Start, Stop, and Replay the Demo

If you want to give the learner more control over the demonstration, you can use Dreamweaver behaviors to control when the demonstration starts, stops, and restarts.

Viewing the Finished Exercise

Before completing the steps for this exercise, take a look at how the page should look when you are done with this exercise.

On CD: Open and explore /*sample_2*/*sample_2-8.htm*.

Creating Learner Demo Controls

In this exercise you will create a **Start**, **Stop**, and **Restart** button that will let the learner control the demonstration.

To create controls that allow the learner to start, stop, and replay the software demonstration, follow these steps:

1 Using Dreamweaver, open /sample_2/sample_2-8_start.htm.

Note: This file begins where the last exercise left off. If you successfully completed the last exercise, you may want to use your own file instead.

2 In the Dreamweaver document design window, insert the image /sample_2/startbutton.gif just after the paragraph of text (Insert → Image).

3 Also insert images stop_button.gif and restart_button.gif.

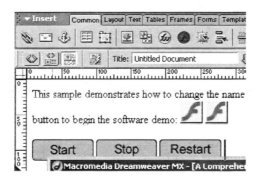

4 Select the Start image and use the Behaviors panel to attach a Play Timeline behavior (Timelines → Play Timeline). Choose the only timeline on the page.

5 Change the event to onMouseUp.

6 Select the Stop image and use the Behaviors panel to attach a Stop Timeline behavior (Timelines → Stop Timeline). Choose the same timeline.

7 Change the event to onMouseUp.

8 Select the Restart image and use the Behaviors panel to attach a Go to Timeline Frame behavior (Timelines → Go to Timeline Frame). Choose the same timeline and enter a *1* in the **Go to Frame** field.

9 Change the event to onMouseUp.

Adding this Go to Timeline Frame behavior will restart the timeline, but the layers that are displayed at the end of the timeline are still showing. We need to hide them.

10 Select the Restart image and attach a Show-Hide Layers behavior and hide all layers except the *mouse* layer and the *MainStage* layer.

11 Deselect the *Autoplay* setting on the Timeline panel.

This ensures that the demonstration won't start until the learner clicks the Start button.

12 Save the file and test the demonstration in a browser.

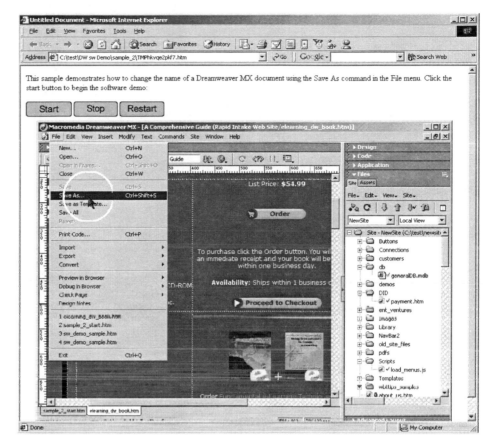

Summary

Sometimes it may be better to allow the learner to control the demonstration. In this chapter you learned how to do that with **Start, Stop** and **Restart** buttons. You can easily add timeline behaviors to these buttons using the Behaviors panel. With the **Restart** button you need to remember to hide all of the layers that shouldn't be showing when the demonstration starts.

Appendix A: Optimizing the Demo

As you add more and more elements to the demo (such as highlighting the mouse clicks and annotations) the size of the demo increases. If you are delivering the demo over the Internet and have a potential audience of dial-up users, you can employ several techniques to cut down on the size of the overall demonstration.

Using Cropping to Reduce Total Image Downloads

To reduce the number of large images the learner needs to download to view the demo, make sure to create screen captures of only those elements that you need. For example, in the demonstration you worked through in this book, instead of repeating the File menu image in its entirety every time the mouse passed over an option in that menu, we simply used screen captures of that specific option.

In the current demonstration, we could reduce the overall size by approximately 40k by choosing to display only those areas of the final screen that changed. When the user saves a document as a different name, the only change they will see is the new name being displayed on the title bar and down on the file name tab. So there is really no need to use an entire window screenshot again. We could have just taken two smaller captures, one of the title bar and one of the tab at the bottom and displayed those at the appropriate positions.

Replace this image with images of just the title bar and file name.

These are the only elements of the screen that changed.

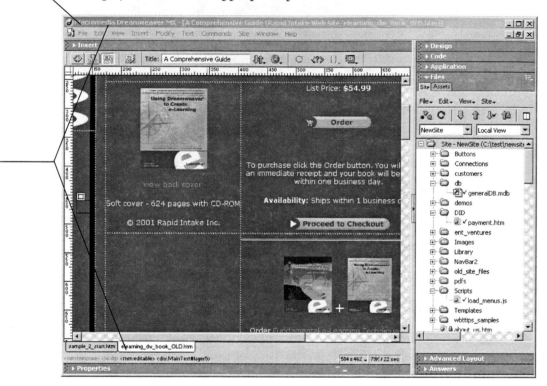

Reduce the Detail

In the demonstration in this book, we used a lot of detail to show what is possible. You may be able to get by without so much detail. Do users really need to see the other menu options highlighting as the mouse passes over them? Maybe not. So you might want to skip it. Instead, spend the bandwidth on things that matter, such as the mouse click highlights where they are needed. The file size ends up being smaller and you save yourself a lot of time.

Optimize the Image Files

Another way to reduce overall file size is to optimize the images themselves. Use Fireworks or another graphic editing program to find the best settings for the smallest possible file size.

 Tip: One way to reduce GIF images is to increase the Loss setting. By changing this setting you can often still end up with an excellent screen capture that is 30–40% smaller in size.

Only Demonstrate the Necessary Area

Don't feel like it is necessary to demonstrate the entire software interface. If the task you are demonstrating can be confined to one small area, demonstrate only that area and make only screen captures of that area.

For example, the exercise in this book demonstrated how to use the Save As feature. We could have made the dimensions of the initial screen shot and the final screen shot much smaller and still illustrated the Save As feature.

Pre-load Images

When you can't make file sizes any smaller and you've made the best judgments you can about what to include and what not to include, make sure to pre-load the images, so that when the demo starts, it runs smoothly.

To pre-load screenshot images, follow these steps:

1 Click the Body tag selector.

The body tag selector lets you select that tag without having to enter the code view.

> sample_2_start.htm | el
> sample_2-8.htm
> <body> <div#MainStage> <img>

2 Use the Behaviors panel to add a Preload Images behavior.

Dreamweaver displays the Preload Images dialog:

3 Click the **Browse** button to select the images you want to preload.

4 Click the plus sign button to add additional images to the list.

5 Make sure that this behavior is triggered by the onLoad event.

Using the Preload Images behavior will ensure that once the learner does start the demonstration it won't be hampered by poor performance.

Relative Size of Demos Created in Dreamweaver

Surprisingly, using the techniques in this book you can create demos whose final file size is comparable and often smaller than using other tools that are designed specifically for creating demos.

To get a rough idea of the file size different tools output, we created the same demo, without the audio, in using various tools on the market. This table lists the final file sizes of each approach and their corresponding format. It is sorted in order with the smallest file size displayed first:

Authoring Tool	Demo Size	Format
TurboDemo	148K (with Java Resource files) or 754K SWF	Native or SWF
Dreamweaver	169K	Native HTML

Authoring Tool	Demo Size	Format
ScreenFlash	170K	SWF (choppy video)
TurboDemo	178K	SWF
ViewletBuilder	264K	SWF
Camtasia	270K	AVI (requires plugin)

Of course, one of the biggest advantages to using Dreamweaver as a demo creation tool is the fact that it does not require a plug-in, and, if you're reading this book, you probably already have Dreamweaver and don't need to pay for another tool! Overall we have been impressed with Dreamweaver's ability to create smooth animations that require no plug-in.

Index